A Sack Full Of Blood

A Sack Full Of Blood

Michael Lee King

THE REGENCY PUBLISHERS

ISBN: 978-1-957724-71-3 (Paperback Edition)
ISBN: 978-1-957724-70-6 (Hardcover Edition)
ISBN: 978-1-957724-72-0 (E-book Edition)

Book Ordering Information

Phone Number: 315-537-3088
Email: info@theregencypublishers.com
The Regency Publishers, US
www.theregencypublishers.us

Printed in the United States of America

Contents

Prologue 7

Chapter 1

The early years 9
The Northern Plan 11

Chapter 2

The Apostle From The South 25
I'm Gonna Tell My Daddy 36

Chapter 3

The Road To Redemption 41
The Flat Tire Miraculously Inflated 48
Safety In the Tree..49
Healing In The Water...50

Chapter 4

Church at Philadelphia.......................................51

Chapter 5

Lord Save My People Back To The South 53

Chapter 6

No Place To Call Home But Emmanuel............65

Praying Women On The Move:
The Little Church On The Hill.................70

I can't go back home without it! 75

Don't Let It Be Everlasting Too Late 79

Chapter 7

Labor Pains Of Church Growth 84

A Pastor Amongst The Flock.........................84

An Example Of Christ In Our Lives.......................88

Get Out And Don't Come Back: This Is God's Hospital....91

I am depending on God 94

Expanding the Kingdom of God:Growing Pains 96

There Must Be Something To It 97

The Baptist Tradition Problem 98

The Confusion Problem........................99

Seeing is Believing........................102

The Night I Received the Indwelling Holy Ghost 104

Chapter 8

I Have Finished My Course A Miracle Even In Death...110

The Alcoholic Demon Cast Out 119

About the Author.................123

PROLOGUE

Greetings, in the precious name of Jesus Christ. Here, I want to tell you why it was necessary for this book to be written. The narrative of this story is true and real as experienced, witnessed and told by the men and women discussed herein, many of which left this life not too long after recording their part in His story. This is a book that records the historical remembrance of a time in American, Southern, African American and religious society when the word of a woman meant less than that of a man even if she was merely repeating and carrying a message given or spoken to her by another man.

Of course, this is not an idea, custom, or phenomenon peculiar only to America, the South, African Americans or the Christian Church. For, the roots of gender discrimination and punishment of women has its genesis in man's original sin in the Garden of Eden and the woman's punishment for actively presenting herself as an emotional, visual and audible stumbling block to entice her husband to commit and follow her into sin. The problem is not the punishment of the woman, but rather the male's unjust, unholy and unrighteous interpretation and application of the wife's punishment, as it relates to the relationship between the wife and her husband—to applying it to all relationships between a male child and a female child. The resulting sin is the sin of *having respect of persons*—a sin so detrimental to the cause of Christ that the gifts and talents born in the female gender, of those who are created in the image and likeness of Christ, are stunted, shunned, many times cast aside and forbidden to the point that, a cause that is already short of laborers is even made less effective because of the intentional teachings to place no faith or belief in the words of a female ambassador.

If we listen only to the male voices who teach for doctrine of Christ and the apostles, the hatred of having respect of persons against women in working for God, then one might be persuaded to believe that God, the creator of all things and of the female of our species, makes a mistake every time he endows, gifts and ordains women, in the womb as he does the male child, to perform his will as well as, as faithful as and many times better than many men of their generation. Of course, these men are wrong and on the wrong side of the word of God. For, God is no respect of persons and in Christ Jesus there is neither male nor female. There is no male spiritual calling or female spiritual calling of God. For God is a spirit and all that worship him must do so in spirit and in truth without regards to gender.

Therefore, it was necessary to write this book as eye witness proof that God will indeed forgive and make whole a runaway twelve-year-old boy and cause him to perform mighty acts in His name for His cause. And that, he likewise will indeed forgive and make whole again a runaway twelve-year-old girl who, before being introduced to Him personally, laid down and bore ten children out-of-wedlock. But then, after receiving His indwelling spirit into her physical body as a leader and her guide, chose life over death and walked away from her nine living children that she might have a chance to live again. But, she did not stop there, she preached, taught and planted many churches for her new Love Christ Jesus, in the same spirit as did the twelve-year-old runaway male servant of God. And God, being a rewarder of them that diligently seek him, made a way for the female servant to have her children taken care of as she took care of His.

Chapter 1

THE EARLY YEARS

The year was 1946, one year after the war had ended in 1945. The Germans were defeated. The world had planted the seeds of a one world government by creating the League of Nations that later became the United Nations. A world, governmental organization with nation membership, the League and later the United Nations was man's way of keeping in check the rogue nations and leaders around the globe. The headquarters eventually settled in New York, New York, United States of America.

From this backdrop of world affairs, we find situated in a livable, quant apartment house in the city of brotherly love, Philadelphia, Pennsylvania, a devout and dedicated servant of the living God of Glory. The same God that had brought to an end World War II, by allowing the Allied forces to be victorious in the deliverance of and the liberation of millions of death camped Jews, waiting on their extermination by a ruthless and godless leader in the person of Adolf Hitler.

This woman of God was born Hattie Mae Caldwell, one of twelve surviving children of Ed and Dora Caldwell. Having grown up in the South, in a little hamlet called Cleveland, North Carolina, it is believed that Hattie Mae Caldwell attended the Old Hart School in Woodleaf, North Carolina, as did her brother-in-law Hezekiah Luckey. This Hart School for Negroes was located on a deep, back country, dirt road, in a part of Rowan County that had no indoor bathroom facilities, no indoor plumbing, no indoor running water and no electricity. Although this old, run down, barely useable, dilapidated, wooden shack was woefully lacking as a proper venue for the task of educating young minds, Hattie Mae would later come to see this old school in a more glorious and meaningful way later in her life.

While in school, and later as a Southern, female Negro, Hattie Mae acquired and consciously nurtured the northern itch, an itch packed full of deep social implications for the survival of freed Black folk that so many African Americans of her day had been stricken with. This itch needed to be scratched, and, as many of her kind thought back in the day, the only way to scratch this itch effectively was to set her hopes and aspirations on a rumored, better life in the Northern states. You see, the Northern states are the part of these here United States of the Americas that had fought long and hard to set her fore parents free from the chains of a slavery so brutal and inhumane that the God of Glory set White brothers against their White brothers and White fathers against their White sons, in a mighty move of salvational deliverance of the Negro.

By causing a sword to divide the houses of the White brothers and the White fathers and their sons, the Lord God ushered in judgment upon an economic, social, cultural, religious and legal system that regarded a portion of God's precious children as not fully human—only 3/5's of a man. The wrath of God was so great, and the deliverance of Hattie Mae's fore family so profound, that it resulted in the total and utter destruction of the Southern, genteel way of life, along with the sacrificial deaths of more than an estimated seven hundred thousand plus souls for the cause. Much blood was shed for the salvation of the Negro.

THE NORTHERN PLAN

Hattie Mae Caldwell, having begun traveling with well to do American Jews across the United States, for non-field work, decided on a plan that would accomplish two goals, save her pre-16-year-old daughter from herself and change her residence permanently from the South to the land of opportunity in the North. This plan would scratch and soothe that Northern itch, yet it was rather simple having come into full bloom at the most needed time. For, Hattie Mae, at this time was no longer Hattie Mae Caldwell, but had gone through a separation from her Common Law cohabitation with James Luckey and married a tall, handsome and gentle fellow, a Mr. Earl Grier, from Charlotte, North Carolina. And, by now, after having naturally birthed twelve children of her own, including four boys: Percy, James, June and Floyd, along with eight girls: Christine, Eldora, Louise, Geneva Mae, Leola, Johnsie, Delphine and Hattie, Momma Hattie Mae had become well versed in the proper methods of protecting her offspring. In between Hattie's travels she had learned that her daughter, Geneva Mae, had been secretly seeing a young fellow named Willie Key, rumored to be age 18. Geneva Mae, about to celebrate her sweet-sixteenth birthday thought that she was in love. And, as Momma Hattie Mae was told, Geneva Mae was planning to elope with her newfound love to South Carolina, where they could 'Say I do', without Momma Hattie Mae's consent. But as surely as Momma Hattie Mae had repented of her own wayward, sinful ways and was now a Southern, Negro, female, Gospel preacher, she was having none of this nonsense from her seventh child.

Momma Hattie Mae thought about this thing. And now, being a woman of God devoted to the salvation of souls, she chose a course of action that would save her daughter from the dastardly, life ruining mistake of running away from home, just to be with a boy. Geneva Mae was a curious, friendly, talkative, loveable and beautiful, countrified, Black girl. She had been endowed with a silky-smooth, dark-skinned complexion that was bountifully draped with long, flowing, loose curled, black hair. God had a plan for her later in life. But as of yet, the seventh child of Momma Hattie Mae had not yet learned that youthful lust, a lust that for many centuries had paraded around as love in the hearts, minds and physical bodies of the young, had never put food on the table, bought clothes for the family unit or provided a home for the lovers to lay in. No! Geneva Mae was definitely too young to grasp the horrors and heartache that would assuredly follow such an uninformed, and uneducated chosen path in life. She was now about to make a choice at the most precious and perilous crossroad, in her short sojourns, here, in this world.

Geneva Mae could not be left alone, to wallow in her own, self-destructive vices. She was in need of rescuing. Immediately! But the rescue plan of action had to be simple and unsuspecting, least the industrious and bold youngin' should get wind of it and run off to elope just to spite the plan and the planner. This plan had to be so bland that even her almost sixteen going on 30-year-old daughter would not suspect it until it was too late to prevent its victory. Geneva Mae had to be saved!

Momma Hattie Mae considered that Geneva Mae, like most young people of her age, would love to have a sweet-sixteenth birthday party with friends and family coming from near and far to celebrate her sixteen years of existence. After the party, feeling good about Momma Hattie Mae's giving her this grand party, Geneva Mae would think nothing of Momma Hattie Mae sending her up North, several hundred miles away from Charlotte, North Carolina, to visit with her older sister Eldora, in Philadelphia, Pennsylvania. Maybe she would even think that, after all, maybe my big sister had a special gift for my wonderful and all important, sixteenth birthday also. Then, after Geneva Mae has visited Eldora for a spell, Eldora would let her know that she could not return home. And of course, by being a young black female from the deep, rural South, broke, with no money and no return bus ticket,

Geneva Mae would have to give in and stay in Philadelphia. Give her time and enough space and she will most likely forget and get over her great, infatuated love for Willie Key.

Thus, armed with her plan to save her daughter, Geneva Mae, from herself, Momma Hattie Mae set the plan in motion. The day was October 17, 1945. Not warm, not cold. A regular Fall day in the deep South. But what was warm, was Geneva Mae's excitement about this birthday party and of her secret plans to elope and be with the love of her life, sometime after the party. She eagerly dressed and dolled herself up for the party, with her long, flowing, loose, curly locks of black hair draping her shoulders, while, at the same time, framing her silky, smooth, dark and shiny facial tone, that God had dressed in creases of what seemed to be the most friendliest of smiles. The day was in full swing. Friends and family came and showered her with gifts and congrats. It was such a wonderful, endearing time for Geneva Mae, the seventh child, of a salvational minded Momma Hattie Mae. The party went on without trouble, a hitch or even a whimper of suspicion from the pompous and secretive Geneva Mae. To top the celebration off, Momma Hattie Mae gave Geneva Mae permission to begin officially taking male company at their home. This was just so wonderful Geneva Mae thought. Little did she know that Momma Hattie Mae was one step ahead of her. By giving her permission to take company, the boy would be required to visit her at her home, and Momma Hattie Mae would be there waiting and watching. At least for now, this would slow up Geneva Mae's planned quest to elope. For, it did appear that she had more freedom. But in reality, Momma Hattie Mae's permission forced Geneva Mae to bring her secret affairs out into the light. There would be no sneaking around in the light of home based, supervised courtship.

Geneva Mae was so overcome and excited about her new found freedom until it did not dawn on her, at the time, that Momma Hattie Mae was now not leaving to go to work and travel with the Jews every two weeks, as she routinely did. Nor did

Geneva Mae think it strange that Momma Hattie Mae actually came home for the specific and expressed purpose of giving her a birthday party with gifts and to give her permission to see boys at home, although under supervision. Momma Hattie Mae was a wise mother. She knew her daughter, her secretive boldness and what she was capable of trying in the darkness of an absent, adult, supervised presence. So, Momma Hattie Mae stayed home from traveling with the Jews, beginning the day she arrived for Geneva Mae's birthday party until sometime after Geneva Mae arrived in Philadelphia, some three months later.

Sometime after the party, Momma Hattie Mae, set in motion, the next part of her plan to save her daughter from herself. She suggested to Geneva Mae that her big sister, Eldora would probably like to see her little sister now that she had reached that all important milestone of womanhood—sweet sixteen. Geneva Mae, trying to be the fox, had been outfoxed and was woefully unsuspecting that her elopement plans had been found out. And discounting the wisdom and insight of Momma Hattie Mae, Geneva Mae readily and gladly agreed to go North to visit her sister for a couple of weeks. No doubt she thought to herself and said to her love, Willie Key, I'll be back and we will leave and be together. But little did she know, that the next time that she would be allowed to enter the State of North Carolina, that red-hot flame of infatuated love that was burning with an urgent need to be quenched by Willie Key, her love, would have long faded away.

Several months had now passed with the New Year ushered in, in the dead of winter. On this cold day in January, 1946, Momma Hattie Mae convinced one of her male neighbors and good, family friend to see Geneva Mae off at the bus terminal. She had already schooled the neighbor on the plan to save her daughter from the likes of Willie Key. But before Geneva Mae would be off, Momma Hattie Mae bade her goodbye, instructing her in her usual stern and firm manner to behave, obey your sister and have a good time. And, I'll see you soon my child.

Geneva Mae, real anxious to leave, because the sooner she left the sooner she would be able to get back to Willie Key, hugged Momma Hattie Mae and journeyed to the bus terminal with the family friend. Her new, official, temporary, adult male, rescue worker watched her with a gaze of protection, as was the custom back in the day, to ensure that Geneva Mae actually got on the bus and stayed on the bus. Geneva Mae, still unsuspecting of Momma Hattie Mae's plan, gladly and anxiously loaded the bus. Of course, being Black and in America, in the year 1946, meant that she had to go to the back of the bus. She was Black and by law was not allowed to sit and ride in the front of the bus, even if there were no seats in the back of the bus for her to sit, and there were many empty seats at the front of the bus. So, to the back of the bus Geneva Mae went. Momma Hattie Mae had taught Geneva Mae and all of her children as they became of age, how to mind their manners around White folk. Be polite. Do not cause any trouble. Stay in your place. And on the bus, her place was in the back of the bus.

Geneva rode that segregated, seated bus all the way to Philadelphia, Pennsylvania, enduring the many stops and wait times the bus had to make along the way. When the bus driver finally brought the bus to a parking stop upon reaching Geneva Mae's long-awaited destination, she unloaded herself. And, having fetched her bags, she began looking around anxiously for her big sister Eldora. And oh, there she was. "Geneva Mae!" Eldora hollered. Geneva Mae, hearing first and then seeing her sister, ran up to her while her shiny, flowing locks tumbled down her neck, blowing in the slight, winter breeze that her lively gate had created. When she was spotted, she was found broadcasting the most wonderful, joyous and excited blushes of a young Southern girl. There she was, that girl from the South, standing in a most youthful awe of an international city. This was indeed the biggest city she had ever stepped into. Oh, if Willie could have just been here, the moment would have seemed perfect. But, even without

Willie, it was a fun time. The big city. Big lights. Cars everywhere. So many Black folk.

Geneva Mae settled in for the visit in an apartment house located in the 700 block of West Jefferson Street, Philadelphia. But while truly enjoying the visit with big Sis', she was subconsciously counting down the days when she would return home to Charlotte, to her love, to her Willie Key.

And finally, the big day did come, but it did not end as Geneva Mae had so anxiously planned it. On this particular morning, Geneva Mae arose with an anxious expectation. An expectation that she would, within hours be saying her goodbyes and fare wells to her big sister, Eldora. Eldora, seven years older than Geneva Mae, had followed Momma Hattie Mae's instructions and did what she could to make Geneva Mae's visit a happy and good visit. For, Eldora already knew that what Geneva Mae believed was a short visit was actually the beginning of her new life up North, away from the deep south, Charlotte, North Carolina, and more importantly, away from Willie Key. So, making her stay pleasant and fun, would help later when the day came to inform her little sister that she had been exiled from Charlotte, North Carolina to the city of brotherly love.

After the day had begun to grow older, Geneva Mae, with her anxious anticipation of being homeward bound, popped the question, "Dora do you have my ticket so I can go home?" Eldora, having been a major culprit in assisting Momma Hattie Mae with the plan to save her little sister from herself, quietly, but with a steeled finality in her voice, that Geneva Mae had grown accustomed to, told her little sister, "You are not going home. Momma said that you cannot go back to Charlotte, North Carolina, and for me not to send you back. No, I do not have a ticket for you. And Momma did not buy you one. She will be up here soon. And you can talk to Momma about it." With that said, as if there was no expectation of hearing even a slight, rebuttal response, Eldora, the big sister, vacated the crippling atmosphere in which Geneva Mae's future had just been rerouted into forever.

Geneva Mae immediately realized the implications of the message from Momma Hattie Mae, delivered to her with the voice of her adoring big sister. This same voice that had so many times helped her in life and had been so gracious, kind and hospitable to her during life's good and bad times and especially for the past few weeks, now spoke with authority and with the intonation of someone who intended to make sure that Momma Hattie Mae's message was heeded and obeyed. When the news, that she had just tuned into with her ears, communed with her understanding, it suddenly grabbed her heart, like a stored, old, unused meat grinder starving for new meat to tear apart into a thousand pieces. The time, the place, the moment was like the world had stopped turning and Geneva Mae's heart had broken into many, many, many pieces. Oh! Could such a heart continue beating after suffering such a break up into so many helpless, crushed pieces? How could love feel so good and hurt so bad? Geneva Mae was devastated! For, she really thought that she could not live without Willie Key, her love, her life, her planned future. Help me! Willie, help me!

With the impact of the delivered message from Momma Hattie Mae falling upon her like a ton of love gone cold, twice iced over, Geneva Mae broke down and cried profusely. The heated and heartbroken tears quietly and relentlessly flowed down her dark, smooth, beautifully shaped cheeks, and into her lap. Her smooth skin glowed as the light reflected upon the tiny rivers of crushed love that gently cascaded down the high cheek bones of her broken smile. Her long, flowing, loose curled, black hair draped the tender hands that barely held up her throbbing, heaving, sobbing head, like a widow's black veil attending the funeral for the lost love of her life.

How could this be happening to me, she thought. Upset. Upset. Upset with Momma Hattie Mae, with big sister, with the world. Suddenly her sweet sixteenth birthday did not mean as much anymore. The big city and the big lights of Philadelphia were so far away from Charlotte, the city and refuge of her great love. This city, Philadelphia, seemed now to be her jail on a deserted island in the middle of an unchartered, impassable, endless ocean. It had become her prison possessing walls that were so tall she could not get over them, walls that were so wide she could not go around them. Philadelphia! I hate this place she thought. I'm gonna find a way back to my love, back to my Willie Key.

But, just as Momma Hattie Mae had planned, days began passing by and then the days became weeks and the weeks became months. With each passing day, the distance from Geneva Mae's love seemed to get farther and farther away. And when the distance married time, they two joined hands and initiated the centuries-old process of healing little Geneva Mae's broken heart. As Eldora maintained her understanding, but protective watch over her little sister she noticed that the healing had begun. Geneva Mae was exhibiting obvious signs of the rebound. For, the time had come, when finally, the fountain of tears began its inevitable process of downsizing, followed by the gradual comeback of Geneva Mae's radiant, attention grabbing, Southern, welcoming smile. And so, to, for Geneva Mae, as her sea of tears began to ebb and subside, reality began slowly slipping into her daze of disappointment and self-pity. And with the help of the prayers of a praying mother, back in Charlotte, North Carolina, reality finally took control. She was a Black, female, from the South with only a seventh-grade education at sixteen years old. She was broke and knew no one in the big city but her big Sis' Eldora, and several of her older brothers and sisters who would forcefully, if need be, enforce Momma Hattie Mae's exile of her from Charlotte, North Carolina. They loved her dearly, just as she loved them. But she was stuck. She had no way and no means to see or hear from Willie Key. Most Black folk back then did not have telephones to call and chat. And not many White folk had them either. So, by crying herself to sleep a many nights, the pain of an unrequited love slowly began to ease.

And Geneva Mae's broken and shattered heart slowly began to heal itself.

It was now March, 1946. Momma Hattie Mae had already sent her daughter, Geneva Mae Luckey, up North in January. And by now her little heart was well on the path of healing itself, from such a destructive and dastardly path. So, in March 1946, Momma Hattie Mae, and her husband Earl Grier, followed and headed north, scratching that itch for a better life than the rolling fields of corn, cotton, and sugar cane, that she had become so accustomed to engaging her time in, before she found work while traveling with the American Jews. And there was something else. She had a sixteen-year-old daughter that had been heartbroken, was not in school and was not working. She was just wallowing in the broken pieces of a dreamed about and fantasized future that would never be. Now, up north, Momma Hattie Mae settled in at Philadelphia's 700 block of West Jefferson Street, in hopes of continuing her work for the Lord God, and starting a new life for her wayward, sixteen-year-old daughter. She had to be saved.

Momma Hattie Mae was now at the age of 41. She had been introduced to this world on a cold, dark, Southern 3rd day of April, 1903, as the fourth child of Dora Cherry Caldwell and Ed Caldwell. When Momma Hattie Mae was born, Jim Crow and separation of the races was the culture and law of the land. General Nathan Bedford Forest, in an attempt to deny and resist the judgment of God upon the southern way of life—while existing in a numbing, humbling and bewildering defeat—began the misuse of white bed sheets and white pillow cases. With white bed sheets General Forest made himself a white robe. With the pillow cases he made himself a white hood for his head, to hide his face and identity, with holes cut out for a set of eyes that refused to see any good thing coming from the freedom and manhood of the Negro male. And there was also a hole cut out of the pillow case for a mouth that spoke evil, traducing, lying declarations against the man, the woman and the child whose skin color and pigmentation remained the color of more than three fourths of the world's population.

And then, as the coward that he would soon prove to be, General Forest began wearing his new White supremacist costume—for the purpose of the continued offence, intimidation, harassment and killing of the newly delivered, freed and emancipated Negro. This defeated General, of the vanquished, Confederate States of America, was bent upon making sure that the Lord's newly freed man stayed in his place. This intent resulted in the creation and passage of southern laws that embodied the spirit and intent of the General's post-Civil War weapon, the Klu Klux Klan, a religion and doctrine based upon hatred, bigotry and the idea that White folk are a superior race, and the Negro was not fully human. This was the same spirit and seeds of hatred that Adolf Hitler would harvest in less than eighty years later, before and during World War II, to justify the brutal, murder and slaughter of innocent Jews in death camps, just because they were not pure White folk, but were Jews. The Klan's religion of White supremacy, written in the law of the land of these here United States of America, was called Jim Crow.

With Jim Crow, the Negroes, as Hattie Mae's kind was called back then, had their place and the White folk had their place. The goal was to maintain a false and *'Gone with the Wind'* status quo, that had been utterly uprooted by the Lord God during the Civil War. To do this, everyone had to stay in and maintain their place and station in life. In Jim Crow, it was deemed, taught, believed and enforced by the courts of the land that the Negro was born into, created for and suitable only for the servant class. And the Whites, well, they were the class of people for which the Negro was born for, and created to serve. For, this was the normal, natural and proper order of things, here, in these old Southern States. At least this was the effect of and the intent of Jim Crow and the law of the land. For, surely no one would expect that the darkie that breast fed our children as infants alongside of her own mulatto child, by the master; that planned, prepared and cooked our every meal; that made our clothes, cleared our forests to make planting fields; that built our houses and provided us with such profits that allowed us to lead such a genteel life—would think, desire or deserve, or was created to be the White man's equal, or a concern of the blue eyed god of heaven and earth, that hung on the walls of the White man and the Negro.

But, even with all of this negativism and hatred in the land, little Hattie Mae Caldwell was destined to become a messenger of the Most High God. She would later become the mouth piece of Jesus Christ, whom the good, ole White folk had painted with blue eyes, wearing long, blond, stringy hair, and sporting pale, pinkish tint skin, all in contradiction to the biblical description of Christ that would later be found in Elder Mother Hattie Grier's personal copy of the book of Revelation. Even with this glowing error and intent of Jim Crow to enter into the body and the church of Jesus Christ, by having respect of persons, still yet, Momma Hattie Mae would become His mouth piece unto souls dying in these here Southern and Northern lands.

Now that Momma Hattie Mae had settled in at Philadelphia, she began working on Geneva Mae's new life in the big city. She informed Geneva Mae that she needed to go ahead and enroll in school because she needed her education. But Geneva Mae was now 16 years old and had not yet completed the seventh grade. She wanted an education but she was now too ashamed to go. She informed her mother that to go now at her advanced age with little kids in the seventh grade, the other students would bully and pick on her. She did not want to be picked on or bullied. So, Momma Hattie Mae told her, "If you are not going to go to school, then you will have to get a job and go to work." This arrangement Geneva Mae could live with, so she agreed.

Momma Hattie Mae talked with her Jewish friends about a job for her daughter, Geneva Mae. After the discussions the Jewish family, surnamed Ostinek, agreed to hire Geneva Mae as a live-in nanny, housekeeper and cook. She would live with them as a part of the family and the Jews would take care of her. Momma Hattie Mae told them plainly, "Do not abuse my daughter. If you cannot handle her, then you send her back to me." They understood and agreed to the work, financial and living arrangements. And so, Geneva Mae went to stay with the Jewish family and worked for them. While there, she took care of and helped raise the family's two boys who were of the approximate ages of twelve and six, when Geneva Mae started working for them. Geneva Mae kept the house clean and they taught her how to clean and polish the furniture and the silverware in the manner that they preferred it. Since they were practicing Jews, they did not allow any form of pork products in their home. So, to ensure that Geneva Mae was able to cook and prepare the types of foods that they desired to eat as Jews, they taught her how to prepare Jewish food. Geneva Mae, quick and eager to learn, soon became very efficient in her new job and in the preparation of Jewish cuisine.

The Ostinek family was really good to Geneva Mae and treated her as their daughter. They even required of her to inform them in the event that anyone should say or do anything to her inappropriately. Geneva Mae really enjoyed living with that family and the wonderful vacations and trips to Atlantic City, New Jersey. The mother did not work, but the father had a very profitable antique business. They were very wealthy and owned a home in Atlantic City on the beach. Every year, when the boys were out of school for the summer months, starting in June, the family would spend the summertime in Atlantic City when the beaches were beautiful. The people that Geneva Mae met were very kind to her. The family made her stay, with them, feel like home to the point that after a while Geneva Mae forgot all about Willie Key—the boy that her whole soul, body and mind had once thought, was the love of her life.

She was having so much fun living and traveling with the Jews, until her emotional state healed itself to the point that she seemed to be unaware of Willie Key. No! There was no time to think about Willie Key. She was having too much fun. And so, with no time to think about him, as the months rolled by, the day came when finally, there was no place left for him in her heart. Time and distance had robbed Willie Key of his special and once exalted place in her heart. Willie Key had become a distant, unemotional memory of a time in her past that was totally unimportant to the present and not suitable or qualified to be considered for a bright future. Momma Hattie Mae Grier, the praying, preaching mother of twelve children from North Carolina had won. Geneva Mae's life had been changed forever. She was not yet saved or complete for the Lord's work, but she was saved and removed from the ditch and the clutches of Willie Key and the dastardly life that she had errantly set her heart on living. This was a life that Mother Hattie Mae was too familiar with. And the pitfalls were so devastating that she was determined to prevent her own children from falling blindly therein.

After Geneva Mae left North Carolina in January, 1946 it was more than a year before she was allowed to return to North Carolina. And, after she said goodbye to Willie Key in 1946, she saw him only one time after that and it was more than a year later. When she finally did see him there were no sparks, no flame and no desire. The fire had been completely extinguished. There was no need to call Momma Hattie Mae's fire department of observation, because there was no smoke to observe and no fire to put out. It was all over. The love that Geneva Mae thought she had and thought that she could not live without, was gone. No longer did she tingle at the sound of his name. No longer was there a fuzzy feeling in the bottom of her stomach when she thought about not being able to see him, or the sick feeling when she realized that she could not get to him. It was all gone. Even the 'what ifs' had vanished from her thoughts without the slightest regret. Yes, it was gone. Oh my! How awesome is the power of prayer from a praying mother, led by the Spirit of God?

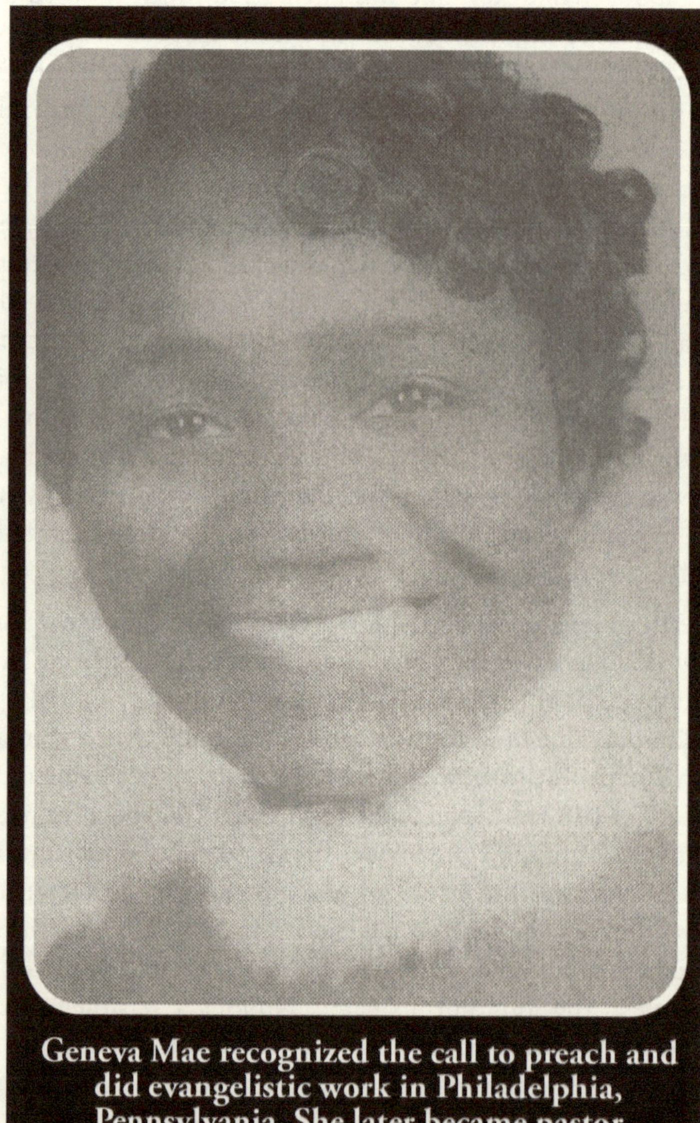

Geneva Mae recognized the call to preach and did evangelistic work in Philadelphia, Pennsylvania. She later became pastor of Mother Grier's church in Philadelphia, after Mother Grier's death

Chapter 2

THE APOSTLE FROM THE SOUTH

Before Momma Hattie Mae made the decision to relocate and move to the city of Philadelphia permanently, she had already started a church for the Lord in Charlotte, North Carolina with another female minister named Hattie McAfee. The church that Momma Hattie Mae and Hattie McAfee started in Charlotte, North Carolina was called St. Peters Apostolic Church, located on Spratt Street. They had been assisted in this work by Bishop Leroy R. Mills, and so the church became a part of the religious, organizational work that Bishop Leroy R. Mills was engaged in. Bishop Mills' work was also called St. Peters Apostolic Church. Bishop Mills was recognized as being the first preacher to bring the apostolic, holiness standard in the name of Jesus to these parts of North Carolina, and to many parts of the State of Florida, during the first few decades of the twentieth century.

When he first came back to evangelize North Carolina Bishop Mills was known as Elder L. R. Mills. His normal disposition was that of a quiet, humble and soft-spoken man. He was not a preacher that sought out recognition, adulation or glory. Nor was he a proud dresser. His dressing style was one of modesty and plain looking. In his later years Bishop L. R. Mills was of a short to medium height for a man, about five feet six inches tall. And he wore his naturally, curly and wavy hair combed backwards. His skin tone was of a reddish-brown tint. His torso was plump and round. But he was a preaching, teaching somebody.

He was strictly a man for the people, even to the point that after he had established several churches and church houses, Elder Mills would be found sitting out in the audience with the lay members until it was his time to preach or teach. He was a man that shunned fancy material things including fancy cars.

On one occasion one of his church members, Sister Margaret Murdock, was desirous to see her pastor drive around town in a fancy, big Cadillac car like the cars the other pastors in the city were driving. So, Sister Margaret ventured to ask Bishop Mills, "Why don't you drive a nicer car than the years-old, second-hand cars that you always drive." Bishop Mills, in an attempt to teach the young maiden not to fall in love with the world and worldly things, said to Sister Murdock, "If I wanted one of those Cadillacs or fancy cars like the other pastors drive, I can get me one. But I do not desire that." He went on to inform her that his interest and his treasures were not of this world. His love and his interest were in Jesus and God's people. For, the Word of God teaches us to,

15 Love not the world, neither the things that are in the world. If any man love the world, the love of the Father is not in him.

16 For all that is in the world, the lust of the flesh, and the lust of the eyes, and the pride of life, isnot of the Father, but is of the world.

17 And the world passeth away, and the lust thereof: but he that doeth the will of God abideth for ever.

1 John 2:15-17.

Bishop Mills was born Leroy R. Mills. When he talked, his voice sounded like he was talking through his nose, and so his voice had a nasal quality to it. At the youthful age of 12, Leroy Mills decided to run away from home to be on his own. During this time, he lived with his mother, a very religious woman who oftentimes would speak in tongues. Leroy did not understand what was going on with his mother. So, one day without telling her of his plans he thought that he could sneak out of the house and run away without his mother knowing it. So, Leroy packed the few clothes that he owned into a little sack. He tied the sack on the end of a stick and slipped out of his mother's house at about dusk dark. His plan was to sneak into the woods quickly without being seen and be on his way. But, as he was walking towards the wooded forest his mother hollered out at him, not to make him stop, but to bid him a more proper farewell and sending off. To his surprise she said to him, "I'll see you in heaven." Stunned by her goodbye, Leroy slipped on into the woods, into the night and into a life all alone on his own at the tender age of 12. He thought that he had gotten away from the influence of his mother's prayers. But little did he know, the Lord was not yet ready to let go of Leroy Mills.

After diligently searching, he finally found a job working on the railroad tracks for the railroad. Later on, he developed a taste for whiskey and began drinking alcoholic beverages. On one occasion with his whiskey bottle in his back pocket, as a young man, Leroy sat out walking to meet up with a friend to go and perform a job. Only this job was illegal, could end in his death or could end in a long-term prison stay. But the spirits found in the whiskey bottle has been known to remove the greatest of inhibitions from the minds and hearts of many great men. And Leroy, still a young boy, was no exception.

On this day, Leroy and his friend had taken the time to plan a bank robbery. Leroy was due to meet up with the friend. So, on his way to meet the friend he decided to cut across this big field which was a cow pasture. Out in the field was also a little wood framed building that was being used by a back country Pentecostal congregation as a church and meeting place. On this late afternoon, when Leroy crossed the fence to walk across the field, he heard the joyous praises coming from the little wooden church. Leroy tried not to notice what was going on, in the church, because he had in his back pocket a whiskey bottle with whiskey in the bottle, and a plan in his mind to get paid the easy way—rob a bank and take other people's money.

Leroy continued walking and as he came closer to the little church a voice spoke to him and said, "Go into the church and see what they are doing." Leroy had not been interested in what they were doing. All he was interested in at the time was the contents of the whiskey bottle and meeting his friend to go and rob the bank. But, after hearing the voice, he hesitated a little and that hesitation was enough to allow him to consider obeying the small still voice that he heard beckoning him to go inside the little church.

So, with the whiskey bottle in his back pocket, Leroy walked up to the church, removed the whiskey bottle from his pocket and hid it under the church steps, for safe keeping and later pickup. Because, in his mind, his intent was to return and fetch it and finish off the contents later. After placing the bottle, Leroy ventured on into the church and sat on a seat in the back of the church. The praises were very much alive and the anointing in the atmosphere was high. Then, after a little while one of the older church women came to the back, where Leroy was sitting, and said to him, "Why don't you come up to the front." She was very kind and friendly. And Leroy, not wanting to offend or disobey church folk obeyed and left his 'at the back of the church seat' vacant and walked up to the front of the church seating area and sat down.

Sitting in the front made the praises of the church members seem even more joyous. These people were really enjoying themselves. Then one of the sanctified church women said to him, "Why don't you kneel down and pray." And again, in an attempt to be obedient to this church lady Leroy knelt down on his knees and began praying. Not long after he began reciting a prayer that he had learned years ago, about repentance and forgiveness he went out under the anointing of the Holy Ghost, speaking in another tongue. Leroy revealed later that while he was out, he was caught up within this huge light while at the same time he was speaking in tongues. The tongues were such that he had no control over what he was saying, nor did he know what he was saying. After remaining in this state for several hours, while the church members stood around and watched, Leroy stepped out of the light and came back to himself. And when he was finally able to recognize where he was, it was between 2 and 3am in the morning. Leroy had been out under the power of God for hours. On this night that he received the indwelling Holy Ghost, his plans had been to go and rob a bank.

Leroy, the changed young man, was now anxious to go and find his potential bank robbing friend and tell him all that had happened to him. So, he went to his friend's house and spilled it all out, rehearsing what the Lord God had done for him. What he did not know at the time was that his older friend had once received the indwelling Holy Ghost and had backslid and gone back on the Lord. After Leroy had rehearsed the nights events, he informed his friend that he could not go with him to rob the bank, because God had changed him, his mind and his heart. He no longer had a desire for the whiskey bottle or for gain illegally gotten. Leroy's friend became very agitated, irritated, mad and angry with Leroy because of Leroy's sudden move from a life of sin to a life of peace. The friend still wanted to go and rob the bank. But Leroy refused. He was a changed young man.

The friend's wife, concerned that her husband was being too mean and harsh towards Leroy said, "Don't get mad and angry with him just because he has turned to the Lord." And, from that moment forward, Leroy lived a life of virtue and faith, in his walk with Christ, before his friend to the point that Leroy's life encouraged his friend to return to the sheepfold and come back to the Lord Jesus.

Momma Hattie Mae came to know Bishop Mills while he was holding services in Rowan and Iredell counties situated in the western back woods of the Piedmont of North Carolina. Bishop

Mills was originally a native son of the area and had much family there. But, later in life he journeyed to the State of Florida and adopted it as his home. After receiving the indwelling Holy Ghost Brother Mills was under the tutelage of Bishop Gregory, a oneness, Apostolic, Pentecostal preacher, who was also reported to be a trained lawyer in the law. He worked and learned under Bishop Gregory and later went out from Bishop Gregory and began evangelizing the South using the oneness, salvational doctrines that he had been taught. At the time Momma Hattie Mae met Bishop Mills he was not yet consecrated as a bishop, but he was a sure firebrand preaching, teaching, Pentecostal preacher, water baptized in the name of Jesus Christ and possessing the indwelling of the Holy Ghost.

During one of his many travels, the Lord Jesus Christ spoke to Elder L. R. Mills telling him that he needed to go home to North Carolina and get his people saved. Elder Mills, obeying the voice of the Lord, made preparations with his immediate family in Florida and the church congregations that he was involved with and began the missionary, church planting journeys to North Carolina. When he first arrived and began introducing the people to the Pentecostal message of salvation there were no buildings or friendly churches for him to preach in, he being a firebrand, Jesus' name Pentecostal, and the majority of Black folk, including his family, being either Baptists, Presbyterian or some sect of the Methodist faith. Unfazed by the daunting task ahead of him, and with a joy to serve the Lord Jesus Christ, Elder Mills began roaming the country side for homes that would let him in to tell them of this life saving, soul delivering, life changing way.

At first, even his family, that he came to save, thought that he had lost his mind or that he was going crazy. They had been good, outstanding, church going folk for years and their preachers had never mentioned to them any of the type of salvation that their son, their nephew, their cousin, their uncle, their brother or their old friend and acquaintance was now teaching and preaching.

They loved him, but they were a very religious, suspicious bunch. But, because of his tenacious, steadfastness and outward sincerity some opened the door to their homes just to give him a chance, to hear him out, and no doubt on some occasions to be polite to a local, home boy who had fared well in life and had come back home to help his people. Little did they know that by opening the door to their homes, they had inadvertently opened the doors to their hearts. For, the Pentecostal message that they heard was undeniably potent. It would either draw you or drive you. And, to the credit of his diligent obedience, many that heard began to believe.

Eventually Elder Mills had gathered enough willing houses until he was able to have 'prayer meetings', as they were called, at a different house each night. By doing this no one house was overburdened and the Pentecostal message was able to reach more people in more areas. During the warmer months the new converts, not having a formal church building, adopted the brush arbor, temporary building concept that had been widely used on the continent of Africa. When it was necessary, the men would cut down pine trees and cut limbs from the trees. Then they would make at least four poles from the trees and set them up for corner posts. Next, they would take the long branches and stretch them across from pole to pole, and fill in the middle parts until the temporary structure had a complete roof over it.

Sister, Evangelist Christine Glaspy Cornelious described it this way: *The brush arbor would not protect you from the rain, because it was not water proof, but it would keep the beaming hot sun off of you. It provided shade. And it gave us a place to go and have church services. Elder Mills would come preach and teach, and the people would come. He was my mother's first cousin. His daddy, Tom Mills, and my mother's mother, Lillie Mills Wilson, were sisters and brothers. And many of our people thought that he was going crazy teaching this new doctrine. But it was all in the bible and we did not know it. He showed us that what he was teaching us was right there in our own bibles. Before he came, we did not know that water baptism in the name of Jesus and receiving the indwelling Holy Ghost were in our bibles. Elder Mills went all up into Statesville, Rowan County, Charlotte and the surrounding areas of North Carolina, preaching and teaching the name of Jesus and the holiness standard. The first church that he ever built in North Carolina was located in Ellenwood, an unincorporated hamlet halfway between Cleveland and Statesville off of US Highway 70 West.*

The brush arbor method worked well for a long time. It was all that we had. People were leaving the Baptist, Methodist and the Presbyterian churches, and coming to hear this new doctrine. Elder Mills had married Evelyn Davidson. It was reported that her family owned about 150 acres of land in the Ellenwood area. And so, since Elder Mills was preaching and getting people saved, his wife's family, the Davidsons, gave him the land so that he could build what became his first church in North Carolina. The church, called Emmanuel Tabernacle, was built using pine logs. People back then did not have much transportation, so many of them road on the back of a big truck from the Cleveland, Amity Hill and Bear Popular areas of Rowan County, North Carolina, just to be in the service at the new Ellenwood church.

The next church that Elder Mills built was located in Statesville, North Carolina and was pastored by Elder Johnnie Smith, and the third church was located in the Amity Hill community of Mt. Ulla, North Carolina. The Statesville and the Mt. Ulla churches were also called St. Peters Apostolic Church.

Elder Smith married Elder Mills' cousin, Jessie Wilson. Elder Smith had come to the Lord and gotten saved under Elder Mills' ministry, and he had been pastoring the Statesville church. Before the church political troubles started, Elder Smith began the building project of the Amity Hill community church with Elder Mills as his spiritual leader. By this time there were two other bishops working with Elder Mills in the church organization, named Bishop Smith and Bishop Cutler. They were all living in Florida and the name of the organization was Southern Emmanuel Tabernacle Apostolic Church. The other two bishops decided to take over the work that Elder Mills had started in North Carolina and it ended up in court. Everyone knew who had performed the work. It was Elder Mills. But it seemed that they just could not get alone. It is reported that they eventually sold the church in Statesville. The Amity Hill community church had been built by Elder Smith and he was the pastor. But once the confusion and trouble started, he did not want to be a part of the confusion. So, we stopped fellowshipping with Elder Mills' organization, to avoid the confusion. With a need to continue in the faith, the church became a part of the Emmanuel Pentecostal Church of Our Lord of the Apostolic Faith, Inc. organization. Years later St. Peter's Apostolic Church in the Amity Hill community became known as Smith's Chapel, Emmanuel Pentecostal Church. And, during Elder Smith's declining health, partly due to being over worked, Minister Walter Chambers was elevated to the pastorate of the church, and he eventually became the Southern Diocese Bishop of the Emmanuel Pentecostal Churches until 1974.

In 1974 Bishop Walter Chambers broke off the formal, organizational ties with the Emmanuel Pentecostal Church organization and took with him the congregation and the church property known as Smith's Chapel, Emmanuel Pentecostal Church. On December 3, 1976, Bishop Walter Chambers founded another church organization naming it the Saint Paul's Pentecostal Church of Our Lord of the Apostolic Faith. And after a fire destroyed the original church located in the Amity Hill community, Smith's Chapel's congregation split with a portion going with Bishop Chambers to build a new church off of US Highway 70, on Sandra Avenue, in Cleveland, North Carolina. The new church is called New Smith's Chapel and in the year 2013 is pastored by his son, Bishop David Chambers. The old Amity Hill location was rebuilt by the remnants of the Smith Chapel congregation and is now pastored by Bishop Arthur Wayne Brown, nephew of Sister Christine Cornelious and cousin of Elder Leroy Mills. The Amity Hill location is called Smith's Chapel Apostolic Holiness Church.

When he started the prayer meetings Elder Mills was determined to reach as many souls as he could and tell them about the salvational plan as found in the Holy Bible, Book of Acts, chapter 2 and verse 38, which states,

Then Peter said unto them, Repent, and be baptized every one of you in the name of Jesus Christ for the remission of sins, and ye shall receive the gift of the Holy Ghost.

Elder Mills' work was very significant during this time due to the decades of domination over the spiritual lives of Black folk, since the end of slavery, by the Southern Baptist, the Methodist and the Presbyterian faiths. And neither of these sects of the Christian faith believed or taught that the plan of salvation, for mankind, was found in Acts chapter 2, verse 38. Furthermore, none of them baptized their converts in the name of Jesus. Although they were Protestant churches that rejected the leadership and many of the doctrinal teachings of the Roman Catholic Church, headquartered in Rome, Italy, they all continued to follow the baptismal ritual set out by the Roman Catholic Church in 225 B.C., wherein the titles father, son and Holy Ghost were spoken over the baptismal candidate rather than saying the name of Jesus, as the New Testament Apostles had done.

So, Elder Mills' mission and goal was to prove by scripture and to convince all that would lend a hearing ear to his 'house on fire' urgent brand of preaching and teaching that to baptize a person in the name of Jesus, is to have baptized them in the name of the father and of the son and of the Holy Ghost. One might wonder why any of this mattered so long as the convert believed in Jesus Christ as their personal savior. But Elder Mills set out all over the countryside in these here Southern States to show that if the Lord Jesus Christ has commanded that a thing should be done, then when the convert comes to the knowledge of the requirement to do or to perform the thing that should be done, then it becomes sin when the convert knowingly refuses to obey the commandment. And, as what must have been mentioned many times, *'No sin shall enter in the kingdom of heaven.'*

The commandment that the teaching Elder so tirelessly championed for the cause of Christ and that caused so much fuss and anguish amongst the leaders and pastors of the Southern Baptist, Methodist and Presbyterian churches is found in Matthew, chapter 28 and verse 19, wherein it states

Go ye therefore, and teach all nations, baptizing them in the name of the Father, and of the Son, and of the Holy Ghost:

When viewing Matthew chapter, 28, verse 19, it is obvious to the reader that it is in fact a commandment. The Elder went around driving his beat-up, years-old, second-hand automobiles with its may-pop-anytime tires, and parking it wherever it was initially allowed, informing the people that to obey Christ you did not have a choice to do what the scripture says or not to do what the scripture says. To obey the command of Christ as found in Matthew 28:19 above, the person who was actually performing the baptismal service of the convert had to use the one name that represented the name of the father, the name of the son and the name of the Holy Ghost, all at one time. In his teaching, Elder Mills let the people know that if they had been baptized before, with the titles of father, son and Holy Ghost, but had not been baptized in the name of Jesus, to obey Christ, it was required that they be baptized again in the name of Jesus.

It was hard work trying to un-teach what was considered by Elder Mills to be religious error committed by unknowing preachers and what was un-apostolic in its origin. Elder Mills had developed this position after years of reviewing the actions and customs of the Apostles in the early church as found in the Holy Scriptures. He discovered through studying the Word of

God that, in the first church, not one preacher or Apostle used the titles father, son and Holy Ghost when baptizing converts. But, in every instance mentioned in the bible, after the day of Pentecost, every convert was baptized in the name of the Lord Jesus Christ.

This uncompromising, unapologetic, fiery brand of preaching and teaching did not gain Elder Mills many friends. But, as was his way, he did not come to make friends but to deliver the apostolic message of salvation in the name of Jesus. He came to warn, to admonish, to save and to deliver. And, it was during these 'house on fire' prayer meetings and teaching services that Momma Hattie Mae, who had been raised up in the Baptist faith tradition, decided to change her life and live for the Lord.

From the age of twelve, when she ran away with her lover who stole her away from home, up to this time, she had been looking and searching for true love; searching for that something that could totally fulfill that yearning deep down in her soul. She had never personally experienced the indwelling power of God at her home church, Mt. Zion Baptist Church, Borden Quarters. But now, finally she had found it. It was all so new, so wonderful, so life changing, coupled with an inner peace that was beyond description. It was Jesus indwelling her on the inside.

I'm Gonna Tell My Daddy

After Momma Hattie Mae was baptized in the name of Jesus and received the indwelling gift of the Holy Ghost, she was anxious for her family and children to be saved also, to discover this inward, indwelling peace. So, she arranged with Elder Mills a time when he could baptize her four oldest children. On the day and at the appointed time and place, the people came and gathered around the creek bank for the baptismal service. Others came to be baptized on this same day that Momma Hattie Mae had brought her children to be baptized. Elder Mills baptized Momma

Hatttie Mae's oldest two children, Percy (Boy) and Christine, and her fourth child, James (Luckey), without any problems. When it was time for Eldora, Momma Hattie Mae's third child, to be baptized, Eldora hesitated and did not want to go down in the water to be baptized. Eldora was afraid of the water. And, up to this point no one actually knew how terrified and fearful Eldora was of moving water flowing across her face. But eventually, even with the almost mentally paralyzing fear that had begun to grip her mind and therefore her soul, Momma Hattie Mae was able to convince Eldora to go on into the water.

Eldora was around seven years old at the time. After she had nervously and anxiously waded into the sandy brown colored water, Elder Mills gently, but firmly held on to Eldora. He had seen her around with her Momma and the family and he knew that she was a scrappy, little maiden. So, while firmly holding her, Elder Mills brought Eldora down, completely under the water, while saying, "I baptize you in the name of Jesus." She was completely buried in this watery grave. But little Eldora was having none of this dunking her head and her body under the water. She was not a fish, and this water was not her grave. She was alive, not dead. And, as if to prove the point, as her head entered the water, and the water buried her entire body in its sandy brown, wet and watery coffin, Eldora did not wait for the patient Elder Mills to resurrect her out of it. She assisted in her own resurrection process by wiggling, twisting, turning, raising and pushing herself up out of that 'water in my face' grave. Then, without thought, concern or consciousness as to the consequences of her actions, Eldora, literally, with the energy of a feisty, wet, little kitten on a sugar high, came up out of the water in an excited, agitated, frightened and angry rage.

Something had taken a hold onto Eldora, but it was not the good Lord of Glory. Eldora began to fight Elder Mills in an attempt to make him let her go and turn her loose. She had lost it! Her manners, her respect, and what little self-control she had brought with her, it was all gone and washed away in that 'water in my face' grave. In her mind, she had had enough of this baptismal stuff—*this dunking somebody's head under the water like that*. And then, in a moment of pitching a childish tantrum, Eldora hollered out at Elder Mills with all of the childish indignation that she could muster, telling him, "I'm gonna tell my daddy on you. You put my head under that water!" She was so disgusted until she was ready to involuntarily draft her absent father into a fight that he cared nothing about.

But, until he got there, she was determined to take care of the problem herself. Eldora resisted and fought Elder Mills so violently until Momma Hattie Mae was forced to wade down into the creek and pull Eldora away from Elder Mills. Then she pulled her out of the creek, up the creek bank and onto dry land. There she was all wet and angry and now ugly and mad, with her face frozen in a tortured looking frown. For the moment, this little maiden was through with the man of God and everyone else.

Momma Hattie Mae was solemnly surprised, disappointed, embarrassed and shocked at her daughter's outright disrespect for the baptismal service and for the man of God. And to give Eldora a hint of the depth of her embarrassment and disappointment she said unto Eldora, "You went down a dry devil, and you came up a wet devil." She was right. Eldora was not ready for the idea or the practice of doing the right thing. She had her own mind about things and for now and many years afterwards those things did not include God. At the tender yet rebellious age of seven, no man was going to wash that out of her by just putting her head under the water. But, that 'washing out' fight would come much later in her life. And come it did. Rebellion and the crippling mental fear of the water lost on the day of Eldora's repentance and deliverance. It just took a sack full of blood—belief in the blood of Jesus.

Leroy R. Mills, the 12 yr. old run away,
became a great evangelist, pastor, teacher,
church planter and bishop for Christ. He
was great help to the women laboring in the
Gospel of Jesus Christ.

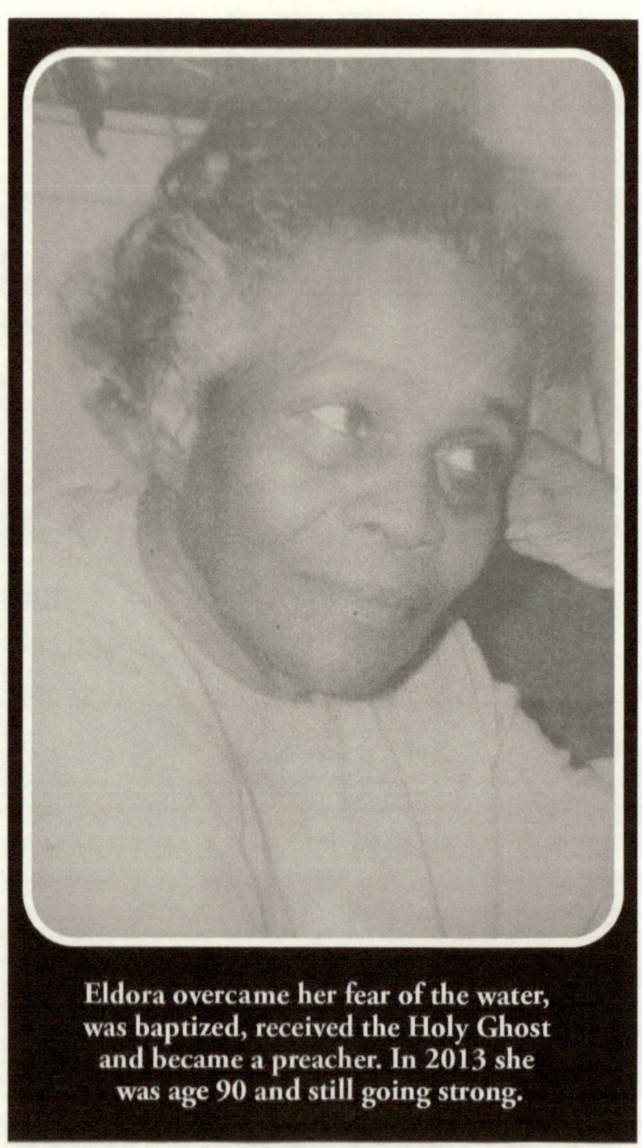

Eldora overcame her fear of the water, was baptized, received the Holy Ghost and became a preacher. In 2013 she was age 90 and still going strong.

Chapter 3

THE ROAD TO REDEMPTION

Momma Hattie Mae's way was hard at first, having run away from home with her grown lover, James Luckey, at the tender age of twelve. After James stole her from home he took Little Hattie with him to Winston-Salem, North Carolina, where they lived together for a while. Between the years 1917 and 1918, at the age of 12 or 13 years old, Little Hattie had her first child and named him Percy. These were hard times. She continued to stay with James and had nine more children while living as his non-State sanctioned common-law wife. The problem was, as everyone else knew, the State of North Carolina did not honor or recognize people living together as common-law husbands and wives. For the cohabitation to be legitimate and for the children to be recognized as legitimate and not bastard children, there had to be a marriage certificate and some authorized person had to perform the marriage ceremony. But James Luckey was his own man. And he was not concerned about these things, such as bastardry, marriage or husbandry.

After giving birth to ten living children with her unofficial common-law husband, James Luckey, when Geneva Mae was a mere five years old, Momma Hattie Mae separated herself from James Luckey. She left him with the nine oldest children. When she left, she carried with her only the eleven-month-old, arm-baby, Delphine. The neighbors and the family did not understand how a woman who had been raised to do better and knew to do better could have ten children and walk off and leave nine of them with a father that was not capable of caring for so many children alone. This was very hard on the children. But, after all was said, rumored and done, the community folk, nor did the children know the truth behind Momma Hattie Mae's seemingly unconscionable act. The truth, that they did not know, was revealed years later, by the father, James Luckey, himself, only after the children became of age.

James Luckey, in setting the record straight, with an obvious pain of conscience after so many years of silence from him, and ridicule suffered by Momma Hattie Mae, revealed the depth of Momma Hattie Mae's love for God over all else and above everyone else after she met Jesus. James Luckey revealed that, Momma Hattie Mae had begun attending and participating in the prayer meetings and teaching services that were being held by an apostolic, holiness preacher named Elder L. R. Mills. Elder Mills had been holding services in and around a little hamlet called Mt. Ulla, which sits adjacent to the Town of Cleveland, North Carolina and adjacent to another little hamlet called Barber Junction. While attending the church, revival like services, Momma Hattie Mae chose Christ to become her personal savior, and to live her life for him.

After repenting of her running away, her disobedience and her wayward ways she was baptized in a local creek in the name of Jesus. She later received the indwelling of the Holy Ghost with the evidence of speaking in other tongues following. Having repented of her sins and with a determined mind to live for the Lord Momma Hattie Mae, with a loving heart, confronted her male companion, James Luckey, about marriage. She informed him that she was now saved and if they were going to stay together and sleep together, as in the past, they would have to get married. But James Luckey was not hearing any of that marriage stuff from her, his babies' mama. So, James, not wanting to be tied down with the vows of marriage, and all that was attached to such vows, informed Momma Hattie Mae that he did not want to get married and that he was not going to marry her.

Momma Hattie Mae was extremely disappointed and dismayed by the attitude and the response from James, a man that had stolen her out of her childhood and had taken her away from her family just so she would be his, all alone. He even moved her miles and miles away to prevent all interference from her large and protective family. While in his care she willingly and gladly with a childish curiosity laid down for him and birthed ten healthy, vibrant and alive children. And now, he was talking to her as if she had just been his play thing, not someone that he respected. She had been a thing that he had used for his sole pleasure and deviant gratification. Even so, she still loved him.

However, she was now in love with Jesus Christ even more. For, now, the Lord Jesus was living within her. Everywhere she went he went. Everywhere she laid he laid. And everywhere she walked he walked. Jesus had become the center of her life, her attention and her day dreaming thoughts.

With a sadness and much concern for the father of her children, the man that had taken her on this wild, youthful and sinful whirlwind ride from childhood to womanhood in such a short time, she uttered the fateful words that would forever change her life. In summary, she told James, "Well, if you will not marry me, then I cannot stay here with you any longer. I will have to find another place for me and the children to live. I cannot continue to live like this and serve the Lord."

To James, a man who had remained in control from the time he boldly stole her from her father's house, now felt the need to stand up to this little woman. It was time to put her in her place, to set her straight and to let her know who runs this house. He had to stand up and protect his manhood. And in doing so, he uttered the ultimate words of fear, dread and tyranny that have broken the will of a many women who dared to become mothers in this life.

His words were shamelessly dreadful, callous, disrespectful, heathenish, barbaric, hurtful and abusive all at once. His words possessed a singular design intended to tempt the faithfulness, the depth and the sincerity of Momma Hattie Mae's newfound love and devotion for her new, live-in lover, Jesus Christ. For, he had moved in. And, he lived within her. It was the first of many tests that Momma Hattie Mae would have to endure and overcome, in order to perform the work for which the Lord God would have her to do.

The test was a simple one. And at the same time, it was a gut wrenching one. It was a test wherein she would be required to choose Christ and live without the benefit of living with and raising her precious ten children. Or, she could forget Christ and remain James' live-in lover, with the benefit of living with and raising her precious ten children. And now, test time had arrived. Would she pass or would she fail?

James Luckey, feeling the tension and the passion of her desire to raise her children, to be with her children, and to serve her newfound indwelling lover, in summary, said to her, "Hattie Mae, if you ever leave me, you had better not take my kids. And if you do take my kids, I will get my shotgun. I will find you and kill you!" James was so sure of himself. He uttered the words in a deliberate, 'I am your master' fashion—with a reckless abandonment, that was heartless and mean spirited. It was like a hot, feverish, longing love gone cold. Momma Hattie Mae was stunned! How could this man say such a thing to me? But regardless as to the answer, Momma Hattie Mae believed that he meant what he said. She knew him and what he was capable of doing. He had defied her father, Ed Caldwell, her mother Dora, her brothers and even the law by stealing her away to be his lover. With her being so young, twelve years old at the time, she had no ability to consent. She had no ability to understand the perils of the dastardly path of life that he was offering her at the age of twelve. He took advantage of a child that had been caught off guard nursing a disobedient mindset.

So, with the threat of death staring her in the face, and knowing that she would only die from within with him and her children, Momma Hattie Mae chose life. She chose to live for Jesus and He in her. With the dread of a mother not knowing what shall become of her children, she quietly began gathering a few of her personal things. The confident James, so sure of himself, still did not believe that she would leave her children. She birthed them through great pain and despair. She loved her children. He knew that about her. She had been a devoted mother to her children. And, as if to taunt her even more, James even consented to allowing Momma Hattie Mae to take the arm baby, Delphine, because she was so small. But even with that he did not believe she would do it. And if she did, it would be only for a little while—just for a couple of days.

But what James did not know was, Momma Hattie Mae was not being led by the emotional attachment to her children as a mother. She was being led by the urgency of the knowledge in knowing that if she did not leave, she and her children would die in sin, and be eternally lost. She knew and believed that someone had to maintain the faith and the hope in knowing that the Lord will eventually work everything out, bye and bye. With a last breath of resolve, Momma Hattie Mae gathered up the baby Delphine and her grab bag of rags and walked out of the door of James Luckey's heart; out of his bed and out of his life. She moved out of the cotton and bean field country of Rowan County and made her new residence in Charlotte, Mecklenburg County, North Carolina.

Daddy James Luckey

(Later in life)

After arriving in Charlotte, Momma Hattie Mae developed and nurtured a habit of going back home to visit with her children every Friday to check to see how they were faring and whether their father James was properly caring for them. During her weekly visits Momma Hattie Mae combed and styled the girls hair; washed their clothes and generally made sure that things were going okay with them. The children were always glad to see Momma Hattie Mae when she came. But it was a hard and difficult way to survive and make ends meet. This arrangement worked itself out after a while, when upon visiting she learned that James Luckey had begun to run around with his friends and other women, and neglecting the children while doing so. So, to solve this problem, Momma Hattie Mae began to take one child away at a time and place them with her brothers or one of her relatives, until all of her children, except for the baby Delphine, were being taken care of by someone else other than herself or their father James Luckey.

Sometime later Momma Hattie Mae met a friendly, nice and kind man, named Earl Grier. She married Earl Grier. And yet still on fire for the Lord, Momma Hattie Mae became known as the preacher, Mother Grier. As Mother Grier she and another, short, small framed, 'fire-brand' woman preacher named Hattie McAfee preached out and started a church in Charlotte, North Carolina. The church was called St. Peters Apostolic Church, after the churches that Bishop Mills had founded. This lively, Apostolic, Pentecostal church was located on Spratt Street. Mother Grier was the pastor and Minister Hattie McAfee worked with her. These two Hatties worked and preached in these here Southern cities where not too many believers or non-believers were willing to sit and listen to a woman preach. But Mother Grier, when she finally came on the Lord's side, stayed there and was determined to obey him and to do his will.

The church congregation that Momma Hattie Mae and Mother Hattie McAfee started still prospers in the Lord and is known today as The Glorious Church of God, the Living, of the Apostolic Faith, Inc. The church congregation was incorporated in 1967 by Mother Hattie McAfee and, at the time of this writing, is pastored by Bishop Robert Lee Huey, Jr. The church congregation later moved from Spratt Street to 3600 Jessie Avenue, Charlotte,

North Carolina, during Mother Hattie McAfee's lifetime. After Bishop Huey began pastoring, the City of Charlotte purchased the Jessie Avenue location and the congregation moved and developed a new location at 304 Statesville Avenue, Charlotte, North Carolina.

Having worked with Bishop Gregory the then Elder L. R. Mills also worked with an organization called the Southern Emmanuel Apostolic Church. In this organization he worked with Bishop Smith and Bishop Cutler in the State of Florida. During the early fifties there was a separation of the churches and Elder L. R. Mills caused the St. Peters Apostolic Church organization to be incorporated, and he was elevated to the office of Bishop.

Bishop Mills founded, started or helped start churches in many States and at one time, it is reported that his St. Peters Apostolic Church organization had churches in almost every city and town within the State of Florida, where his work was headquartered. The Lord blessed the churches in its mission of saving souls. There were pastors in every church. There were evangelists, teachers and prophets and many other spiritual gifts operating in the churches during Bishop Mills' lifetime. And Bishop Mills was always ready to travel and assist the saints and the pastors of other churches.

The Lord Jesus did a mighty work through the labor of Bishop Mills' life, and performed many noted miracles to assist him in his work for the Lord.

The Flat Tire Miraculously Inflated

One noted miracle occurred one night when Bishop Mills and several of the saints were traveling to perform the work of the Lord. They left home with no spare tire and with may-pop-anytime tires on the car. While they were riding on the highway the tire blew out and went flat. It was at night and they were many miles away from the closest place where they could purchase a replacement tire. Bishop Mills got out of the car to check the tire and prayed while he was outside. He got back into the car and prayed more and the saints in the car were praying also. He got back out of the car, went around the car to where the flat tire was and kicked it. There was no bounce and the tire was still flat. Bishop Mills got back into the car and they prayed again. He got out and kicked the tire again with the same result. After several more times of praying and then checking the tire by kicking it, with the same results, Bishop Mills and the saints prayed one final time. Bishop Mills got out of the car, went around the car to where the tire had been flat and kicked it. But this time it was different. The tire had been miraculously fixed and repaired and had been inflated without any human intervention other than prayer. Bishop Mills kicked the tire and his foot bounced off of the tire, because it had been inflated. The saints glorified God for his miraculous work and they continued on their journey home while riding on the repaired tire.

SAFETY IN THE TREE

Another noted miracle occurred while Bishop Mills and his band of saints were traveling to Ohio to deliver the lifesaving doctrine of salvation in Jesus Christ. They were riding on the highway in a car and going around this steep mountain road. Somehow the car ran off the road and went airborne over the side of the mountain. Anyone witnessing the event would have thought that the car's passengers were about to meet sure death and destruction at the bottom of the mountain's ravine. But the Lord Jesus was on their side, and caused a big tree to catch the car as it went airborne, preventing the car from crashing down the mountain side and sparing their lives.

HEALING IN THE WATER

One day Bishop Mills received a telephone call from Pastor Hattie McAffee. Pastor McAffee was the pastor in Charlotte, North Carolina that was pastoring the church that Mother Hattie Grier had left in her charge. Pastor McAffee had a group of young people that wanted to be baptized. So, she called Bishop Mills in Florida and requested that he come to North Carolina and baptize her people. At the time that she called for his assistance Bishop Mills had been under the medical doctor's care and was still nursing a broken leg. The medical doctors had placed his leg in a cast so that it would heal. The leg was not yet healed, but Bishop Mills, mindful of the Lord's work, agreed to travel to North Carolina anyway and perform the baptisms. When Bishop Mills arrived in Charlotte, North Carolina the broken leg and the cast did not stop him from going into the water to perform the baptism. After he had performed the baptisms, Bishop Mills came up out of the water. And once he was completely out of the water, he felt the healing that had taken place within his body. He could actually feel that his leg was now healed. The Lord had healed him while he was in the water performing the baptisms. Excited about his healing, Bishop Mills located a cutting tool and cut the cast off of his healed leg. The leg was no longer broken, and so he no longer needed the cast. Oh, the grace and power of the Lord God.

And, finally, after serving and leading God's people, Bishop Leroy R. Mills departed from this life in 1975. He was 79 years of age.

Chapter 4

CHURCH AT PHILADELPHIA

After arriving in Philadelphia, Pennsylvania in March 1946, with her beloved and supporting husband, Earl, Mother Grier, as she was now known in the church community, soon set out to organize a meeting place for the routine and regular worship and gathering of her family for the performance of the work of the Lord God. Her first attempt to start a church mission in Philadelphia, Pennsylvania was in her house. Several people began attending and Mother Grier soon began renting a little place, for church worship, on the corner of Six and Popular streets in Philadelphia. When Mother Hattie Grier started the church mission, she was the only person in attendance, at the church, that was saved. So, she began having Sunday school teaching sessions every Sunday and she taught everyone that came.

Not long after being in Philadelphia Mother Grier met another woman preacher and they joined together working to get people saved and baptized in the name of Jesus. On one occasion, in particular, they tarried around the altar with a young man named Robert O. Doub until he received the Holy Ghost. Robert Doub's salvation later proved to be a great blessing to Mother Grier and her work in the Lord. For, since the women preachers helped him to find Christ, he returned the favor by being a 'help in time of need' for the women preachers.

Robert Doub worked for the Lord and eventually became a pastor of his own church and became a great bishop in the Apostolic, Pentecostal church movement. Bishop Doub was a fine and helpful man of God. More importantly to Mother Grier was the fact that he had no problem assisting and coming to the aid of women who were bold enough to labor in the gospel. Bishop Doub had a large flock of saints who met on the first floor of a two-story building that he owned. Bishop Doub was married and had three children, two boys Michael and Joel, and a daughter, named Daffney. They lived on the second floor of the building that housed the church, which was named Shiloh Apostolic Temple.

After Mother Grier had been working with Bishop Doub for quite some time Bishop Doub did a wonderful and blissful thing for Mother Grier and her small but growing congregation. He purchased a larger building for his church and gave Mother Grier the building that had housed his church and his family as a gift. This day was a wonderful day and a monumental encouragement for the young church congregation that Mother Grier had started. Now, they would have a real church building that could seat many more people. It was obvious that God had his hand in the work.

Chapter 5

Lord Save My People Back To The South

Later on, as the years began to pass by, while helping to get others saved and into the church, Mother Grier became increasingly concerned about the souls of her kinfolk down South. Most of them were members of Shady Grove Baptist Church and Mt Zion Baptist Church, Boyden Quarters, both located near the Cleveland and Mt. Ulla communities in North Carolina. Finally, as it was for Bishop Mills decades earlier, this concern became a call from the Lord to go South and to work to get her people saved.

During the latter half of the year 1957 Mother Grier began a new church mission on Marshall Street, Philadelphia, Pennsylvania. And during this same time of the year, she was also asking the Lord to save her people that were down South. After much prayer Mother Grier was moved by the Lord Jesus to journey to North Carolina so that God would save her people who lived there.

Mother Grier had already been going down South to visit her kinfolk and her sister, Edna Cowan. While she was visiting, she would conduct prayer services at her sister Edna's house and other people began to come and participate. Sister Edna wanted Mother Grier to come down and conduct a revival at her home church, Shady Grove Baptist Church, so everyone could hear this life changing doctrine of salvation that she was teaching. Mother Grier informed Sister Edna, that Edna would have to get permission from the church's pastor for her to come and conduct a revival, since it was his congregation in addition to the fact that there were many people who did not believe that a woman should preach. Sister Edna's husband, James Cowan, was one of the deacons in the church and she had much family attending the church also, including the head, church deacon, Deacon Ray Ferrens who was Mother Grier's brother Ralph's brother-in-law. The two of them were married to sisters, Annie Belle and Ora.

Desirous for Mother Grier to come, they approached their pastor, Reverend Daniels, and asked him about Mother Grier coming down from up North to conduct a week's long revival at Shady Grove Baptist Church. After consultation and consideration, Reverend Daniels agreed to allow Mother Grier to conduct the revival. So, a date was set for the revival during the latter part of the year of 1957. Mother Grier, a woman, Pentecostal preacher was going to preach and conduct a week-long revival at the Shady Grove Baptist Church where many of her kinfolk were members of the congregation. Mother Grier made all of her necessary arrangements, and, while obeying the Lord, Mother Grier, chauffeured by the daughter of her rescue, Geneva Mae, journeyed to North Carolina to conduct and preach this momentous, weeklong revival at the Shady Grove Baptist Church.

Shady Grove was located in deep, back country, Cleveland, North Carolina. The county is Rowan. And this area of the county was filled with cotton fields, tomato, bean, squash and cucumber fields. It was a place where a large portion of the Black population, that was employed, lived and worked in farming operations. Shady Grove was a church where the people could be saved, many of the members believed, without changing their lives or their lifestyles. And Mother Grier, hoping to see them in the after-life was determined to introduce them to a salvation that was life altering.

At the time of her arrival, her sister Edna's husband, James Cowan, was a deacon, and Ray Ferrens, was a deacon. But there was a problem. None of them, except Sister Edna, possessed the Acts 2:38 salvation that would make them whole and complete in the Lord. Mother Grier began on a Monday night preaching what was scheduled to be a five-day, soul saving revival. The first miracle of the revival was the fact that, in 1957, the Baptist churches as a group did not believe in or allow women preachers in their pulpits to preach. Although knowing this before she left Philadelphia for North Carolina, Mother Grier was determined to help the Lord Jesus Christ save her people.

She arrived at church on a Monday night and was able to preach to a good crowd, teaching and warning the people that to be saved they had to obey the commandments of the Apostle Peter as found in the Holy Bible, Book of Acts chapter 2, verse 38. This was definitely new and novel to most of the people in this Baptist church congregation. Because, Acts 2:38 requires that to be saved, a person must first repent of their sins. And this meant that they literally had to change the way in which they lived. Second, Acts 2:38 requires that to be saved a person had to be baptized in the water in the name of Jesus Christ for the remission of sins. And thirdly, this Acts 2:38 passage of scripture requires that to be saved a person had to receive the gift of the Holy Ghost. And, of course this was totally new to these professing, saved Christians that were attending this Baptist church.

This Baptist church required that to be saved, and therefore to be a preacher to preach, a teacher to teach or a deacon to serve, a person need only to be baptized not in the actual and literal name of Jesus, but in the titles of the father, the son and the Holy Ghost. And the final requirement was to say and recite with one's mouth a variation of the scriptural passage found in the book of Romans chapter 10, verse 9, which states,

**That if thou shalt confess with thy mouth
the Lord Jesus, and shalt believe in thine heart**

**that God hath raised him from the dead, thou
shalt be saved.**

It was assumed that if the person recited this passage of
scripture, then they had already repented of their sins, at least
by the time they had finished saying the words. And with this
assumption came the very public, and vocal acknowledgement
by the preacher, to the salvational candidate, that he or she was
'saved', because they had repented of their sins as evidenced by
their having openly recited the Romans 10:9 passage of scripture.

The problem with this manmade approach to salvation was
that the preacher, nor the pastor could know the person's true
heart and intent. And here, the entire salvational process was
totally dependent upon a third person's belief in the salvational
candidate's affirmation of faith in the Lord Jesus. And so, the
Lord Jesus Christ was left to provide salvation to the salvational
candidates based on the will of man and not the will of God.
Because only those whom the preacher believed and declared was
saved after they recited the Romans 10:9 passage was considered
'saved', which is a contradiction of the scriptures wherein it says,

**12   But as many as   received   him,   to
them gave he power to become the sons of
God, even to them that believe on his name.**

**13   Which were born, not of blood, nor
of the will of the flesh, nor of the will of man,
but of God.**

John 1:12-13.

As a consequence, many in the Baptist, Methodist and
Presbyterian churches were claiming salvation from the very sins
that they had never forsaken and had never stopped committing.
They therefore had never truly repented of their sins in a manner
that was life changing. Jesus Christ had not changed their hearts

or their minds; and therefore, their lives, language, desires and lifestyles had not changed.

Mother Grier, having grown up Baptist, knew and understood the problem that her people faced. They were sincere church going folk, many of them, but they were ignorant of the real, true transforming power of the blood of Jesus Christ that is accessed only through true repentance; and the keeping power of the Holy Ghost which can be received only after true repentance. Mother Grier was determined to bring her people out of this Hell bound ignorance. For, it was the scriptures that declared,

My people are destroyed for lack of knowledge
Hosea 4:6.

And,

13 Therefore my people are gone into captivity, because they have no knowledge: and their honourable men are famished, and their multitude dried up with thirst.

14 Therefore hell hath enlarged herself, and opened her mouth without measure: and their glory, and their multitude, and their pomp, and he that rejoiceth, shall descend into it.

Isaiah 5:13-14.

Knowing all of this beforehand, Mother Grier boldly walked into Shady Grove Baptist Church and by scripture, preached unto the congregation a Gospel message that contradicted the entire salvational doctrine and position of the Baptist church and the teachings that had been taught by Reverend Daniels, to this congregation. She really had a nerve and the gall.

The pastor let it slide the first night, but on Tuesday night he was not going to let this insult past or continue. Mother Grier, through her preaching and teaching demonstrated her total disregard for the Baptist doctrine of salvation, and openly dismantled it by using the Holy Scriptures. It was devastating to the pastor. He did not understand and therefore did not agree. These people were his members! He was not going to allow any preacher to continue preaching a doctrine in his church to his members that was not only foreign to them, but which was readily and openly causing a division within the congregation. For, there were some who, because they did not want to change their way of living, clung to the doctrine that they had become comfortable with. And there were many others who believed in the scriptures and the doctrine as Mother Grier had taught and expounded on them. Each night after Mother Grier had preached, she made an altar call for all that wanted to be saved according to the scripture, Acts 2:38, and to be baptized in the name of Jesus. And, after the altar call was made, many of the Baptist members made their way to the altar because they now believed what they had heard and they wanted to be baptized and saved according to the doctrinal teachings that Mother Grier had taught, preached about, and convinced them was the true doctrine of salvation that had been taught and practiced by the first Apostles.

Having had enough, Reverend Daniels stood up after Mother Grier had finished preaching and yielded the floor. He said, "This woman cannot continue this revival." He announced to the congregation that Mother Grier would not be allowed to preach at the church anymore because the doctrine of salvation that she was preaching and teaching had caused a division within the church. The members of the congregation began looking around at one another, because some of them really wanted to hear more and did not want the revival meeting to end that night. So, to decide what more needed to be done to remedy the problem, Reverend Daniels called out Deacon James Cowan in the congregation. He told him to gather all of the deacons. And he said, "I will meet you all at your house at 1'oclock tomorrow afternoon for a meeting concerning this." The next day was Wednesday. Mother Grier sat there in the pulpit and said nothing. She refused to comment. Reverend Daniels gave the benediction and dismissed the service. Then he had several words with Mother Grier.

Many of those who believed were concerned about what was going to happen, because they wanted to hear more about this real, life changing, salvational doctrine. Deacon James Cowan, one of the head and most trusted deacons at the church, but also one of the believers in this new doctrine approached Mother Hattie for guidance. He asked her, "Hattie, what are you gonna do?" Mother Grier stated, "I'm gonna do what the Lord told me to do." Deacon Cowan then said to her, "But he has called a meeting and he is stopping the revival. He doesn't want you back." He said, "I don't know what to do." Mother Grier, a staunch and diehard believer in obeying leadership said unto him, "You do what he told you to do. He is your pastor. You obey him. And I am gonna do what God told me to do. He told you to convene the meeting, and for the deacons to meet at your house at 1'o'clock. Then go and do exactly that."

Mother Grier had been staying at Deacon Cowan's house, and later at the house she said to them, "When God is in control of a thing, he will work it out. So, you go and do what your pastor told you to do." The next morning, Wednesday, there was heightened anticipation about the past night's events and the meeting that was scheduled for 1 o'clock that afternoon. Sister Edna and Deacon Cowan had awakened early and a great Southern breakfast feast had been prepared and sat out on the kitchen table to warm and fill the stomachs of the entire household. The smell of the fresh baked, homemade biscuits and the country ham was delightful and very tantalizing to the nose. The more they smelled the food the hungrier they felt. And, on this most anxious morning, the household turned out for a hearty, breakfast meal anxiously hungry. They all waited on Mother Grier before starting to eat.

But Mother Grier had a different idea about the food and what was about to happen. As everyone sat down and was about to eat Mother Grier called a fast and directed everyone to not eat and to turn their plates over. This was not her house, nor her kitchen. And she had not consulted with Sister Edna or the man of the house, James Cowan. But it did not matter. Mother Grier was on a mission for the Lord Jesus, and in her sight, He was the man of the house. The family was stunned. All of this food had been cooked and prepared—smelling up the nostrils of a very hungry bunch. But it did not matter. They believed that she spoke for the Lord, and He had spoken. Sadly hungry, but with a mind to be obedient to the voice of the Lord through his sent messenger, they all slowly turned their plates down and removed themselves from the breakfast table. The fast was on.

Then there was some concern that the meeting being held at Deacon Cowan's house may cause some confusion, being that it was the home where Mother Hattie was staying while she was conducting the revival. So, to prevent her presence from being a hindrance to the meeting, Mother Grier directed Geneva Mae to chauffer her all around Cleveland and Woodleaf, North Carolina, beginning at about 10:30 Wednesday morning, to many of the village people's houses talking to them about the Lord and inviting them out to the revival. She did this even though she knew and was being constantly reminded by others that the pastor had told her not to come back, that the revival was over and would not continue. But Mother Grier was a person of fierce confidence in the Lord Jesus and in his provisions in times when he has directed her to perform a task. It appeared to others that the revival was finished. But her faith in what the Lord had told her and had sent her to do, knew that it was not over. Her insistence and persistence in preparing for the night's service made her appear to be stubborn and even bull headed. Mother Grier knew this, but she was more concerned with obeying the Lord, who had sent her, than what the people thought about how God was performing the work, or whether she appeared to them to be over zealous and stubborn.

Later on during the day on Wednesday, Geneva Mae drove Mother Grier back to Deacon Cowan's house. The time was about 3 or 4 o'clock in the afternoon. Deacon Cowan saw the car coming into the driveway and met Mother Grier at the car. He opened the door for Mother Grier and said "Hattie! Guess what! Guess what! Pastor didn't show up at the meeting. What are we gonna do?"He informed her that everybody showed up to the meeting at the appointed time except for the Pastor. So, since the Pastor did not show up, nothing was done at the meeting concerning the revival. Mother Grier asked, "Why did the pastor not show up?" Deacon Cowan informed her that he did not know why the pastor had not showed up. And, during this time very few people had telephones, including Deacon Cowan. So, without a telephone at the time, he had no means of receiving a message from the pastor. He informed Mother Grier that they waited a long time for the pastor to show up and some of the deacons did try to contact him and was unsuccessful. They did not know where the pastor was.

Now, having accomplished nothing at the meeting and the pastor not showing up, with his whereabouts unknown—there was nothing standing in the way, so Deacon Cowan asked Mother Grier, "Now what do we do?" Mother Grier replied, with a voice reflection of knowing authority, "We are going to have church tonight."

Geneva Mae was standing nearby. After she heard and now understood what her mother, the preaching Mother Grier, was about to do, said in a chastising voice, "Momma! You can't go back to that church. You know what the Pastor said. He said that you cannot preach at his church anymore." Geneva Mae had set her hopes on going home and thought that they would be going home, since the pastor had cancelled the revival meeting. But, Mother Grier, with a fierceness borne from a deeply rooted faith in being directed by Christ Jesus and not by the will of man, threw a verbal stun, grenade bomb at Geneva Mae, saying, "You shut up! I know what the Lord told me to do. And that is what I am going to do. We are going to church tonight and I am going to preach."

Geneva Mae was stunned by the firmness in her tone and did not say another word on the subject. She shut down her vocal cords and immediately dispatched her desire to speak. For, although she was a grown woman of approximately 26 years, she knew when Mother Hattie instructed you to do a thing as it pertained to the work of the Lord, she was steadfast in her commitment to see that the work was done. There was no leeway or means of getting around her for the Lord, short of disrespecting her. You did what she said. For, she spoke with the authority of the scriptures and from her faith that the Lord God was he that confirms the words of his messengers. And there was one thing that Mother Grier was mighty sure of, and that is, she was one of his messengers. This she truly believed, and modeled her life in such fashion that her life became a witness and proof that belief in the blood of Jesus is truly life changing.

And just like she said they would, they did have church at Shady Grove on Wednesday night. The deacons began the service on time and carried it out. The pastor was a no-show. The same thing occurred on Thursday night. And it was repeated on Friday night. The pastor was a no-show. He was out of town and did not return before Mother Grier had completed the revival and the people had been baptized. Each night the service was better and more people came. Many of the Baptist members were on the altar seeking for the indwelling Holy Ghost. By Saturday morning Mother Grier had convinced many of the faithful members from Shady Grove Baptist Church to be baptized in the name of Jesus Christ. Her mission was not to convince them to move their membership from the church, but it was her intent to show them the way to eternal salvation. She wanted them and the Pastor, if he so chose to be so, to be made whole in Christ Jesus as the Holy Scriptures required.

The baptismal candidates were told to meet at the church around 10 am on Saturday morning. By the time everyone had gathered that morning, for the baptismal service, the pastor had already called one of the deacons and informed him what had happened concerning his brother and why he had to leave so suddenly. The deacon that he called was also one of the deacons who were a candidate to be baptized in the name of Jesus. So, this deacon, believed to be Deacon Ray Ferrens, informed the group as to why their pastor, Reverend Daniels, had not been able to make it to the meeting. He told them that during the night, after the Tuesday revival service and after the Pastor had made his announcement, cancelling Mother Grier's completion of the revival, Reverend Daniel's brother became deathly ill. The brother lived up north in one of the northern states, and to make sure that he was present if the brother should pass away, the family got word through to Reverend Daniels and told him that if he desired to see his brother alive, he should dispatch immediately and come up North. So, Reverend Daniels left to go up North, and when he left town, he left in such haste that he failed to leave instructions for his deacons to follow during the meeting.

The deacon informed them that the pastor was still out of town up North. God had worked things out. And now, knowing that there would be no interference, the baptismal candidates proceeded to the creek where they would be baptized.

Shady Grove Baptist Church was located on a long, back country dirt road. There was a fenced-in cow pasture across the dirt road from the church. To get to the creek to baptize and to be baptized, the members, the men and the women, crossed a barbed wire fence. They journeyed through the cow pasture for about the length of a city block to the creek bank. After arriving at the creek bank, they had another joyous church service right there on and around the creek bank. The people were going down in the water and coming up out of the water rejoicing in the Lord. It was a wonderful and delightful time to see these country folk find freedom, peace and true salvation in the Lord Jesus.

Many of the baptismal candidates had already been baptized in the titles father, son and Holy Ghost. They now wanted the fullness. As Mother Grier put it, they were taking on the name of the father, the son and the Holy Ghost, which is Jesus, in the same manner a bride takes on her husband's name. On this baptismal Saturday, Mother Grier caused an estimated 15 or more people to accept the name of Jesus and to be baptized, immersed and buried in the water in the name of Jesus. The roll call of baptized candidates included the head deacons and lay members of the church such as Ray Ferrens and James Cowan. It was truly a glorious time down by the river's bank on that deep South, country day in the year of 1957.

Sometime after the baptism, with her work for this assignment complete, Mother Grier journeyed back to Philadelphia. Geneva Mae, now in awe at the move of God, directed the steering wheel all the way back to their resting places up North. Through her preaching many of the Baptist church members that had been baptized in the name of Jesus also received the gift of the Holy Ghost. And on her return trip home Mother Grier did not forget to thank God for saving her people.

Chapter 6

No Place To Call Home But Emmanuel

Not long after Mother Grier had arrived back in Philadelphia she received a message from the new converts back at Shady Grove Baptist Church in Cleveland, North Carolina. The message was urgent. They informed Mother Grier that the new converts were being accused of causing confusion amongst the members of Shady Grove with their newly found hope in the name of Jesus Christ and their salvation based upon the Book of Acts, chapter 2, verse 38.

Shady Grove's pastor, Reverend Daniels, had now returned to his floundering flock, from his unannounced, unplanned emergency trip to the northern States. Upon his return, to his dismay and total dissatisfaction, the Reverend found his entire congregation had been divided in doctrinal terms. Even more disheartening was the fact that his head deacons and lay leaders had switched sides and were in open opposition to the Romans chapter 10, verse 9 salvational doctrine that he, as the pastor, had taught them and truly believed. Although he did not understand, himself, he being the pastor of the congregation was determined that the confusion was going to stop. He proceeded to let the new converts know that as long as they held to this new doctrine and this new salvation, they were not welcome at Shady Grove Baptist Church.

So, when the new converts called Mother Grier, they asked, "What must we do?" Mother Grier told them to, "Obey your pastor. Reverend Daniels is the pastor of Shady Grove Baptist Church. If he does not want you to stay there and praise the Lord Jesus and talk about the truth, baptism and salvation in Jesus' name, then leave and began holding prayer service meetings in your houses."

So, the new converts chose James and Edna Cowan's house to officially begin holding the new, church mission's weekly, prayer service meetings. The Cowan's house was an easy choice since it was at the Cowan's house that Mother Grier had been holding prayer services before she conducted the revival at Shady Grove Baptist Church. And it was Ivey Lee Cowan's and his brothers' bedroom that the services were being held in.

Although he did not know it at the time, the young and boisterous Ivey Lee, nicknamed 'Billy', the fourth son of James and Edna Cowan, was destined to one day become the pastor of this newly formed congregation. For, Mother Grier had already prophesied the event, to Geneva Mae and others, during one of her many trips to the South working to get her people saved. It occurred one day when they spotted Billy at a distance and Mother Grier said to Geneva Mae, "That boy is going to be the pastor of this new congregation at Woodleaf one day." At the time, Billy, as Ivey Lee was called, was a mere teenager trying to find out what the world was all about. But, Geneva Mae, in a sarcastic and doubtful tone questioned Mother Grier's grasp and understanding of who and what type of person Billy was at the time. And in Geneva Mae's mind she did not believe that Billy would ever pastor anything due to his rebel rousing and drunken wayward ways. In a sign of her disapproval of Mother Grier's prophetic utterance Geneva Mae said, "Ole big head Billy. He's just running around in the streets drinking and carrying on." Mother Grier, unfazed by Geneva Mae's disapproval, disagreement and unbelief in her prophetic utterance concerning Billy, stated, "I don't care what he is doing now, or what he has done. God said he is going to be the pastor of these people."

By holding the prayer services in the Cowan's home, the seeds of Billy's salvation were planted in the same bedroom that he slept in at night. Because, to save him it was going to take a sack full of blood—the blood of Jesus. And it came about just like Mother Grier had prophesied, although Billy would not settle down and obey the Lord until several years after the new congregation had acquired its own building for public worship and had received its first pastor. But, eventually, after the seeds had begun to spring up into everlasting life for him, Billy turned his life to the Lord. In his own words, Ivey Lee testified, saying:

"I was raised up in the house with daddy and momma, (James and Edna Cowan). We lived in the house where they started the church. And they used our bedroom. They used the boys' bedroom to have church whenever they had a church service. After a few years that house burnt down. Daddy, momma and the family had to move to another house. My car was burnt up also and so I had to move to Salisbury, North Carolina so that I could get me a job. I found a job working on the Paul Lawrence Dunbar School that was being built in East Spencer, North Carolina. Of course, now I did not have any transportation because my car was burnt up. So, I went to East Spencer and was able to rent me a room. I was not married then. I worked for about a year trying to get things going again. My dad was always talking to me about being saved and moving back home. Nothing fell in place until after I got married.

So, on May 16, 1959, I married Jaunita Poag. The next day on May 17, 1959 my new bride and I went back to church, the little school house in Woodleaf, North Carolina. My wife and I both went to the altar during the service. I repented of my sins. We joined the church. And my dad, James Cowan, carried me and my wife over to US Highway 70, at Second Creek and baptized us in the creek.

Back then they had three services on Sunday. Ray Ferrens was the pastor at the time. So, my daddy, Minister James Cowan, took us back to the church for the service. I knelt down on the altar and tarried for the Holy Ghost. I did not receive the Holy Ghost at that time. During this time Walter Chambers was pastoring a little, mission church in Mocksville, North Carolina. The building where he held the public services for the worshipping of God in was a one room school house. Pastor Chambers had planned a revival meeting that started on the 26 day of May 1959. During this time Pastor Walter Chambers and I were working on the same job site in Cleveland, North Carolina. We were engaged in building the new West Rowan High School right there in Cleveland. He and I were working with the brick masons. So, he and I went on a fast that I might receive the Holy Ghost during the revival. I went to the revival meeting on that Monday night, May 26, 1959. During the service the Lord Jesus filled me with the indwelling Holy Ghost, speaking in other tongues. This is how I got started on that day. I have been a member of Emmanuel Pentecostal Church ever since that day. My wife did not receive the Holy Ghost on that night. My wife received the indwelling Holy Ghost about two weeks later.

Back then the saints and James Cowan would tarry with you around the altar all night as long as you were seeking Jesus and his precious Holy Ghost. It did not matter who you were if you wanted the Holy Ghost, James would stay there with you around the altar. Then, was unlike today when people will work around the altar for thirty minutes and then they are tired. James Cowan was a great altar worker. He would stay with you at the altar until you received the Holy Ghost, no matter how long it took. I thank the Lord for him, because he would not stop. He was very strong in the work of the altar and trying to help people who were seeking the indwelling Holy Ghost to get it. He would even tarry with you in the middle of the day. It could be 12 noon or 12 midnight. It did not matter. He would stay there with you while you were tarrying and seeking the indwelling Holy Ghost.

I started out as a trustee when the church was in the old Hart Road School house. I served as an assistant Sunday school superintendent under Deacon Ralph Caldwell. I went to Sunday school every Sunday. I helped clean the church and helped with the upkeep—whatever we could do to the old building. I sang in the choir and then later after I started preaching Overseer Jones told me that I should save my voice for preaching. She told me to sing congregational songs and not sing so much with the quartet singing group. This proved to be good advice, because it saved my voice. Later, I was appointed the pastor of the Woodleaf congregation. "

Ivey Lee (Billy) Cowan was appointed the National Elder and then in 1998, at the death of Chief Overseer C.F. Jones Jackson, he began presiding as the General Overseer of Emmanuel

Praying Women On The Move:
The Little Church On The Hill

As an encouragement to the new, church mission at Woodleaf, Mother Grier told them that she would ask the Lord Jesus to bless them with a building for worship service. She informed the new, church mission that she did not have the money to buy them a place, but the Lord would bless them with a place to worship Him in. And the Lord did just as she had promised them, not long afterwards. This was an exciting time for these new converts. But they were not yet aware that their move from Shady Grove to the Cowan's house was the beginning of a great move of God right there in these here southern States.

The Lord God had started a great, life changing work in the everyday lives of these deep South, field hands, cotton, tomato and bean picking share croppers. But now, there was the concern that the new house bound mission had no pastor and no sanctuary for the new congregation to assemble for the public worship of the Lord Jesus. Mother Grier fasted and prayed asking the Lord to provide the North Carolina congregation with a pastor and a building for public worship. She then set out to request numerous ministers to accompany her to North Carolina to help with her people.

She contacted Bishop Ledbetter and told him that she had preached out a mission in her home town in North Carolina and that they did not have a place to worship in. She let him know that she needed help. Mother Grier had hope that Bishop Ledbetter would help her because before he moved to Philadelphia he had a church in Charlotte, North Carolina and Mother Grier worked and fellowshipped with him in the Lord. Also, now that he had moved to Philadelphia, Mother Grier was actually conducting a revival for him at his church located in New Haven Connecticut. Bishop Ledbetter did tell her that he would assist her with the new mission. But it seemed that his help was taking too long to materialize so Mother Grier discussed her concerns and need for the North Carolina mission with Elder Robert Doub, and requested his help. Elder Doub told Mother Grier, "Go on down to North Carolina and find a place, and after you have found the place, you let me know and I'll come down and get it for you." Mother Grier replied, "Well, if I had the money to go down there and find a place, I wouldn't be asking you." Although she was disappointed in his response, Mother Grier considered Elder Doub to be her Godson, because she tarried and prayed with him around the altar and helped him get saved—receiving the indwelling Holy Ghost.

But Mother Grier did not give up. She kept praying and waiting on the Lord. And at the time another woman, Apostolic, Pentecostal preacher named Elder Carrie Francis Jones *(latter to be known as Overseer Elder Carrie Francis Jones Jackson)*, lived in Allentown, New Jersey. This woman of God had a church in Hightstown, New Jersey, and had just recently, in October 1956, founded and incorporated a church organization named The Emmanuel Pentecostal Church of Our Lord of the Apostolic Faith, Inc. Elder Jones was the presiding leader and Overseer of the new organization. Mother Grier and Elder Jones had developed a fellowship through their church work in the Lord. So, once during their fellowship visits, Mother Grier told Elder Jones about the new mission that she had preached out in North Carolina. She told her about the need for a building and a pastor. After Overseer Jones heard of the need, she immediately told Mother Grier that she would go with her to North Carolina and that she would help her. From this point forward, Overseer Jones replaced Geneva Mae as Mother Grier's driver when Mother Grier needed to go to North Carolina concerning church business.

It was the last part of the year of 1957, and during this same year Mother Grier and her Marshall Street, Philadelphia, Pennsylvania church became a part of the Emmanuel Pentecostal Church organization. Overseer Jones appointed Mother Grier as the North Carolina State Mother. And in this same year the new mission, located in Woodleaf, North Carolina, became the first congregation of the Emmanuel Pentecostal Church organization in the South. Now, Emmanuel consisted of a Northern and a Southern Diocese.

After a little organizing and planning their trip, and while excited to be in the service of the Lord, Mother Grier and Overseer Jones set out for Salisbury, North Carolina by way of Highway 29 through Washington, D.C. They were on their way to visit and encourage the young congregation. While in North Carolina they began searching for a building that could be used by the new believers for the public worshipping of the Lord Jesus. Deacon James Cowan was also helping to look for and locate a suitable building. After diligently searching, Deacon Cowan located an old building standing on a hill on Hart Road in Woodleaf, North Carolina. Deacon Cowan gave the information to Mother Grier. Sometime later Overseer Jones drove Mother Grier to North Carolina to see and check out the building. After they had inspected the location, they determined that the building and the land was suitable for starting a church and that it was for sale.

This little building sat up on top of a hill, overlooking the dirt and gravel, Hart Road below. The building consisted of one big classroom and two small rooms on the front end with a hallway leading from the front steps between the two small rooms and terminating at the entry way into the big classroom. The building was completely built from wood except for the tin roof and the glass panes that made up the lights in each window. Jack Moore was the owner of the old Hart School building, at the time. The building was known as the Hart School for Negroes. Overseer Jones purchased the building and the land for the new congregation of baptized believers and placed the title in the name of The Emmanuel Pentecostal Church of Our Lord of the Apostolic Faith, Inc. Before they returned home, the two preachers entered the old school house that had now been purchased for use as a church. And Mother Grier, overcome with joy, began praising the Lord and speaking in tongues to the glory of God in the empty building. The Lord Jesus had done it again. He had answered her prayer.

The Hart School for Negroes was located on an old, unpaved, dirt and gravel, farming road called Hart Road. When Overseer Jones purchased the land and building for use by the newly developed congregation there were no public utilities of any kind in that part of Rowan County. There was no public water or sewer, no telephone service, no electrical service and no natural gas service.

So, when the new congregation held services in the building, it was lit by using sunlight from the windows combined with kerosene lamps hanging from the wood, plank walls. The building was heated by utilization of a pot belly, wood stove that sat near the middle of the floor of the big room in the school house. The two smaller, front rooms were not heated. The stove, located in the big room, was situated so that the metal, chimney, stove pipe rose in the air from the top of the back side of the stove to the ceiling. There was a hole cut into the wood planked ceiling that was outlined with tin. This hole allowed the stove pipe chimney to extend through the ceiling, through the attic, crawl space and through the tin roof to the outside.

Later, after members of the church petitioned God and man for electrical power to be extended to the church on Hart Road, the budding congregation was blessed. The electrical power company went through the time, money and expense to build an electrical power grid from west of the Yadkin River in Davie County, North Carolina to the little church on the hill at Hart Road. After the power was made available, Kenneth Safrit, an electrician, was hired. He wired the old school house so that the people of God would have access to the added convenience that electrical power brings. But, there still was no running water, no well and no indoor restroom facilities. Everyone in need of a restroom had to use the wooden outhouse that had been built on the property.

Yes, this was the deep back-country, back-woods, Southern lands. Since the building site was located in Woodleaf, North Carolina, an unincorporated village, the congregation became known as Woodleaf, Emmanuel Pentecostal Church of Our Lord of the Apostolic Faith.

The Woodleaf congregation at the
Hart Road School for Negroes

It was now the year 1958, the people had a building to worship in, but still no pastor. Prayers were made for a pastor and the two Elders journeyed back to their northern homes. They were well aware of the need to have a person who lived in the area to be the pastor, because the two of them lived more than ten hours away, Mother Grier in Philadelphia, Pennsylvania and Elder Jones in the State of New Jersey. A local pastor would be able to provide a local eye, arm and mouthpiece for the Lord Jesus in the growing of this new, young, zealous, energetic and budding congregation of former Baptist, now Apostolic Pentecostals. By this time, in 1958, many were coming to the prayer services and revivals conducted by or sponsored by Mother Grier and Elder Jones. They were being baptized in the name of Jesus and being saved by receiving the indwelling Holy Ghost.

Edna Cowan, one of Mother Grier's younger sisters, was the first person to get saved, amongst her kin folk in the South, due to Mother Grier's preaching and teaching about salvation in the name of Jesus. Sister Edna had repented of her sins and she had been seeking and was extremely desirous of receiving the indwelling Holy Ghost as is promised in the Book of Acts, chapter 2, verse 38. Her big sister and now spiritual leader and teacher had talked about it, preached about it, and taught so often about it until she was anxious to receive this new indwelling life in Christ Jesus.

I CAN'T GO BACK HOME WITHOUT IT!

Sister Edna was so determined to receive the promised gift of the Holy Ghost until she went over the top and made a promise to all that would listen to her. She told everyone that she was going up North to be in a revival with her sister, Mother Grier. And, she promised them, as if it was a guarantee whose outcome, she had total control over. She promised them that when she returned home from her northern trip she would have and possess the indwelling Spirit of the Holy Ghost.

So, determined to exercise her faith in her sister's teaching and preaching and in the Lord Jesus, and to make good on her promise, Sister Edna Cowan journeyed north to Philadelphia, to be in the revival services at Mother Grier's church. The revival preacher was named Bishop Willie Belle Easley. The year was 1955-1956, and Mother Grier was glad to have her younger sister in town seeking for the indwelling Holy Ghost. Sister Edna faithfully attended the revival services each night and sought out the Lord Jesus, on the altar, for the promised gift. But each night she came away disappointed. And each night she returned with a greater determination to receive the gift than the night before. She grew more and more anxious each night because each night before she had failed to receive the Holy Ghost indwelling.

Finally, it was the Wednesday night of the revival. Edna Mae had tarried around the altar seeking the Lord Jesus and his promise of the Holy Ghost as the Apostle Peter had proclaimed and announced to the world at large and for generations to come, in the Book of Acts, chapter 2, verse 38. For, there, Apostle Peter said that if she would repent of her sins and be baptized in water in the name of Jesus Christ, she would receive the gift of the Holy Ghost. It was free, she had been told, for everyone who would seek after Him. She had sought Him out, but yet she had not received the gift.

By now, Sister Edna was becoming a little discouraged, because, in her mind, she had repented of her sins. She had totally changed her lifestyle. And she had taken on the name of Jesus, by being baptized in his name. Yet, she still had not received the promised gift. She began to wonder what the people back home would think of her and say about her if she failed to keep her promise to them and not receive the gift of the Holy Ghost. She had given them a guarantee, a promise. Up to now she had been known as a woman whose word could be trusted. Would they now call her a fake or worst a liar? Would they believe her in the future?

Edna Caldwell Cowan

(Later in life)

The mere thought of returning home, to North Carolina, empty, without the indwelling Holy Ghost was enough to make this grown, strong and healthy, female, field hand from the South break down in tears. She wanted this indwelling Holy Ghost and she wanted it bad.   She had never wanted anything or anyone so bad. Never had she ever sought after achieving a goal in life so intensely. This thing filled her mind, her thoughts, her day dreams and her days with an excited and urgent anticipation. Sister Edna had become acutely concerned about her soul. She had changed her plans for life. And her new plans did not include to one day awake in Hell. She felt that she needed this thing called the Holy Ghost. She needed Jesus within her every day to help her raise her large family and to be a good wife to her husband, James Cowan. Yes! She was in need of Him. And, she seemed to be so close to getting it, and yet so far away. What was the problem? What was wrong? What else do I need to do? Lord, help me!

After she had tarried and prayed on the altar on Wednesday night Sister Edna left the church on her way back to Mother Grier's house totally disappointed in her success rate on the altar. She felt that she had failed. And after she had settled in for the night she burst into tears, and cried out in the night like a little baby, to the Lord Jesus. She said, "Lord Jesus, I can't go home without the Holy Ghost. I told everybody back home that I was coming up here to receive the Holy Ghost. And, I can't go back without it." In between her sobs and the mighty flow of tears, she kept saying, "I can't go home without it." Sister Edna was so disappointed until she was inconsolable. And after she had cried out to the Lord, for a while, as a little child with much tears, the Lord Jesus gave Sister Edna the evidence that she had been seeking to prove that he had heard her plea. He came and indwelled her while she was in bed crying and Sister Edna immediately began speaking in tongues letting everyone around, and everyone in the house know that Jesus was now on board. Geneva Mae and Mother Grier were present in the house and witnessed the work of the Lord Jesus and Sister Edna's entry into the kingdom of God. It was truly a miracle, and all it took was a sack full of blood, belief in the blood of Jesus.

Don't Let It Be Everlasting Too Late

The next person, living in the South, amongst her kinfolk to be saved because of Mother Grier's witness for the Lord Jesus was her niece, Annie Lee King. Annie Lee was the oldest child of Mother Grier's youngest sister, Ruth Lee Caldwell Luckey. On this occasion, Mother Grier had been admonishing and teaching her kin folk that Heaven was real and Hell was hot. They needed the Lord Jesus in their lives. Sister Ruth and two of her younger daughters, Sarah and Coleen were in a state of repentance and were on the alter tarrying and seeking for the indwelling Holy Ghost.

The time frame was the later part of the year of 1957. Annie Lee had married Nathan King and they had a one-year-old son named Nathan Jr., born on May 29, 1956. The young family did not have their own home and so they were living with Annie Lee's mother, Sister Ruth and her husband Hezekiah Luckey and Annie Lee's eight younger brothers and sisters, Addie Mae, Clinton, Sarah, Coleen, Raymond, Richard, Thelma and Idela. Mother Grier had been conducting prayer services at Sister Edna's house and the group had been traveling back and forth to Charlotte to Mother Grier's former church that Mother McAffee was now pastoring.

But, even with all of the back and forth to house prayer meetings and to various churches, Annie Lee and her husband Nathan were not   interested in being saved during this time. They were still young and having fun. Nathan and Annie Lee were married teenagers, only 19 years old. Mother Grier, deeply concerned about their souls, approached Annie Lee and asked,

"Annie Lee why aren't you seeking the Lord and trying to get saved?" Annie Lee, always respectful to her elders, but equally forthright when responding to their questions, said to Mother Grier, "Aunt Hattie, I'm not ready to be saved right now." Annie Lee turned to walk away. But, Mother Grier, with a firm, admonishing but caring voice said to her niece, "Annie Lee, don't you let it be everlasting too late!" Annie Lee recalled later that Mother Grier's words felt like someone had taken a knife and stabbed her in her heart. She felt an emotional hurt, on the inside, and she became fearful for her future. Then her tear ducts filled themselves to capacity and began overflowing with warm, streams of tears cascading down her high yellow, smooth, glowing cheeks. These tears were uncontrollable, and from that very moment Annie Lee changed her mind about salvation and being saved. Now, she wanted to be saved and she felt that she had to have it.

She recalled that as a little girl she would go out into the woods and into the yard to play alone and then she would talk to God. She would tell him that she wanted to live for him and that if she could get something that would help her and remind her to do right when she thought about doing wrong, she would not do the wrong. Annie Lee had developed this quiet relationship with the Lord after having been carried to church by her aunts when she was a little girl. And now, Mother Grier had introduced the family to this 'something', this thing called the Holy Ghost that a person could receive. If you would only believe in Him, and repent and stop doing wrong, if you asked Him, He would come and indwell you and remind you and help you to do the right thing and live right when your thoughts were to do wrong. This is what Annie Lee had been looking for all of these years. Yes, she had to have this thing called the indwelling Holy Ghost.

Annie Lee King was the second or third preacher to answer the call to preach. She gave live birth to 8 children and of the 7 living in 2013 six of them are preachers including 4 boys and 2 girls.

The night was a revival night and Elder Jeremiah Jefferson, Overseer Jones' presiding Elder, was assisting Mother Grier and Overseer Jones with the services. Annie Lee tarried around the altar and sought out God. And when He finally came and touched her, she became afraid and opened her eyes to see who He was. She did not see Him because He is a spirit. And, she was not able to reconnect to Him by simply closing her eyes again. Later after the service Elder Jefferson said to her, "Annie Lee you were really close tonight. If you had not become afraid when the Spirit of the Lord came upon you, and opened your eyes, you might would have received the Holy Ghost."

Annie Lee, disappointed that she did not receive the Holy Ghost was yet not ready to give up seeking the Lord. Later, while at home at her mother's house, Annie Lee's heart, thoughts and mind stayed on the Lord Jesus and what she wanted him to do for her. And, as her thought focused more intently upon him, she made the conscious decision to have church, with Christ, all by herself, like she used to do when she was a little maiden talking to the Lord.

She broke out with a song, singing, 'What's the matter with Jesus, He's Alright.' Annie Lee had been a serious-minded maiden while growing up and now she was serious about the Lord and desired Him in her life seriously. So, when she sang the words of the song, she put all of herself, her mind, her heart, her desires, her emotions, her strength, her body and her soul into singing the song. For a little while Annie Lee forgot about where she was, who was at home and who might be listening. All she was concerned about was singing her song unto the Lord Jesus. She wanted Him to hear her. She wanted Him in her life. And through her singing to him and praising him with her whole heart, she made Him hers. And after singing several verses of the song the Lord Jesus, whom she had been calling upon and singing to in her mind and in her heart, came to see about her. He took her, in the Spirit, to a place that she had never been before. And when he released her and she came back to herself Annie Lee then realized where she was and what she was doing. She discovered that she was speaking in an unknown tongue and dancing across Sister Ruth and Hezekiah's creaking, old, wood, plank floor.

By this time, Annie Lee was making a great and joyous noise in that old wooden house that the Luckey family lived in. The wooden floor was shaking and the noise was so great until her father, Hezekiah Luckey, ran into the room where Annie Lee was speaking in tongues and dancing for and before the Lord Jesus. Hezekiah, realizing that Annie Lee was speaking in tongues and had just received the indwelling Holy Ghost ran out of the room and ran to his wife, Sister Ruth. Hezekiah said to Sister Ruth, "Momma I believe she got it. Annie Lee just received the Holy Ghost." Sister Ruth hurriedly exited the room that she had been found occupying, by her husband, and entered into the room where Annie Lee was present. Sister Ruth wanted to be a witness to this miracle of the Lord God. And when she entered the room Annie Lee was still speaking in tongues as the Spirit of the Lord had given her the utterance to speak in a new language unknown to her beforehand. Having witnessed this life changing scene, Sister Ruth declared, "Yes, my baby got the Holy Ghost." The presence of the power of the Lord Jesus was so strong in the room until Sister Ruth got caught up in the Spirit and began praising the Lord along with her daughter, Annie Lee. Annie Lee King had just become the first person, amongst Mother Grier's kinfolk, to receive the Holy Ghost while standing in the State of North Carolina, due to Mother Grier's witnessing and teaching about Jesus. Her uncle, Deacon James Cowan, Sister Edna's husband followed after her, and soon many other souls, such as Coleen Luckey, Sarah Luckey, Walter Chambers, Dicey Chambers, Charles Cowan, Lawrence Cowan, Ruth Luckey, the Hunts and the Hunter family members, began receiving the Holy Ghost and were added to the church.

Chapter 7

Labor Pains Of Church Growth

A Pastor Amongst The Flock

Mother Grier and Overseer Jones gathered many of the new converts from the Woodleaf congregation for a three-day, absolute shut-in fast. The three-day fast started on Wednesday, February 19, 1958. The participants drank no liquids and ate no food for three days and three nights. The fast was called for the purpose of asking God to anoint Ray Ferrens to preach the Gospel and make him available for the pastoralship of the new church congregation in Woodleaf, North Carolina. The Elders from the North and the Woodleaf congregation held the fast in the newly purchased Hart Road School house. After the fast was over the two Elders returned to their northern homes and while there they received a telephone call from North Carolina informing them that God had anointed Ray Ferrens to preach the Gospel. Overseer Jones and Mother Grier returned to North Carolina and installed Ray Ferrens as the first pastor of the young Hart Road congregation. From the Hart Road Congregation, the Emmanuel Pentecostal Church's Southern Diocese quickly grew to ten churches and 27 ministers, but not without the trouble, confusion and the misunderstandings that goes along with converting whole families from generations of believing in one particular faith to another.

Ray Ferrens was appointed the National Bishop and later started his own work. He served as the presiding bishop over the Glorious Emmanuel Pentecostal Church, East Spencer, N.C.

The manner by which the Lord Jesus had used strong, pious women to boldly enter Southern Baptist churches in the South in the 1950s and call out a holy and peculiar people unto himself was a miracle itself. Many people left the Baptist, Methodist and the Presbyterian churches and converted over to Apostolic, Pentecostal Holiness. Yet, although many were converted and carried the holiness banner, some of them still held onto many of the unbiblical ways and beliefs taught by the Baptist, Methodist and Presbyterian faiths concerning women preachers, women in the pulpit and women in leadership roles that required them to lead men. It was a simple belief system with simple rules—No women preachers, no women in the pulpit and no women leading men. So, for some of the new converts, accepting the new reality of having a woman as their spiritual leader, would take time and spiritual growth. For, as of yet, as newborn babes in Christ they were not aware of the existence and the power of the scripture where the Lord God declared,

How long wilt thou go about, O thou backsliding daughter? for the Lord hath created a new thing in the earth, A woman shall compass a man.

Jeremiah 31:22.

Emmanuel, the new church organization, was growing and was now in need of National Workers. Mother Grier, while engaged in evangelistic work for the Lord, had been instrumental in starting, growing and developing new church missions in North Carolina, before the Woodleaf, North Carolina congregation was started. These missions included the church that Pastor Hattie McAffee was pastoring and another church that Mother Grier and Bishop Ledbetter worked out together in Charlotte, North Carolina. But, with those other church missions, Mother Grier left them in the care of someone else. This time, with the Woodleaf congregation, she would be around to communicate with the saints and the leadership of the church.

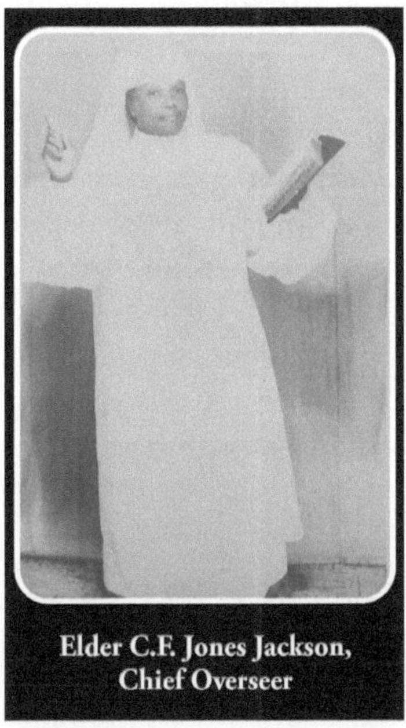

**Elder C.F. Jones Jackson,
Chief Overseer**

**Elder Hattie Mae Grier,
Evangelist**

As an evangelist, preaching out and starting church missions, Mother Grier's goal was to win souls for the Lord and to get the people saved and then to allow someone else to pastor, lead, nurture and grow them individually and as a congregation in the Kingdom of God. On the other hand, Overseer Jones was well suited for the work of expanding the kingdom of God by growing a church congregation into many congregations. For, it was through her teaching and leadership in Christ Jesus that caused the Woodleaf congregation to expand and soon grow from one church congregation to ten churches and twenty-seven preaching ministers. Overseer Jones had a charismatic and loving personality, and an undeniable, and expressive love for the lay people of the church.

An Example Of Christ In Our Lives

Nathan King, Sr., an eye witness from the beginning testified concerning Overseer Jones as follows: *"Out of all of the churches I had been to and out of all of the preaching I had been in and heard, before I met Overseer Jones, none compared to hearing Overseer Jones when she preached or when she taught. Her ways and manners were different from all of the preachers that I had been around. There was something so different about her. I had been around other preachers praying and laying hands on you. But there was something about her preaching—she did not have to lay hands on you for you to feel the power of God. She preached with authority. Just the words that she would preach would touch you without her laying her hands on you.*

And I had never met another preacher with the heart for the people like she had. She would come down to North Carolina from Lakewood, New Jersey just to run revivals for the new congregation. I witnessed many people get saved under her ministry. And when they would go wrong Overseer Jones would not put them out of the church or run them off. She would say, "I'm going to stay with you until you get it right."

One time we went to New Jersey for convention and my wife, Annie Lee, did not have a long coat needed for the cold weather up North. Down South at the time, where we were from, most folk did not own or wear those types of long coats, because they were so expensive. Overseer Jones went out and bought Annie Lee a long, winter coat, and gave it to her. I thought to myself, "People don't just buy other folk coats. This woman is not real." I always said that she was not a real woman, because she was closer to God than anyone else that was in the church in the South. There was not another preacher in the South like Overseer Jones.

In other ways she was like Jesus. She even knew that at least one of the preachers that were in the church in the South was against her and talked against her. She was wise in her communications with the preachers that were not with her. She would say things to them with words that would not make them angry at her, but at the same time she let them know that she knew that they were not with her. And they knew that she knew it.

Overseer Jones would drive from New Jersey to North Carolina just to teach the preachers and the people. This was necessary because the people in the church were ignorant about the Apostolic doctrine of salvation and the holiness standard. She taught the mothers how to be proper mothers to their children and wives to their husbands. She also taught the preachers. She set up and taught a class that consisted only of the preachers to help them. But, although some of them could barely read and write, she helped them and taught them how to develop their sermons and study the bible by searching the scriptures. Yet, some did not appreciate the help simply because she was a woman preacher and a woman leader. If I had continued listening to them talk against women in leadership and women preachers, they would have gotten me mixed up in the confusion also, because, during this time, I did not know what was right on the issue. I had been raised Baptist, and the Baptist did not allow it. I was dumb and ignorant to the Word of God. So, some of the talk almost turned my mind against Overseer Jones just because she was a woman preacher. But then I thought about the issue, thinking to myself that if God was not with her then she could not do the things that she was able to do and gladly did. One thing for certain, I did not know of another preacher like Overseer Jones. She was the closest example to God that I had ever met. I have heard and witnessed people say things to her that were so negative and so bad, that if it had been me, I would have been ready to fight. But, not Overseer Jones—she would just laugh and say, "You know that is not right baby." She never would raise her voice, no matter what you put on her, said to her or done to her. Overseer Jones taught us that when people begin talking to you in a manner that vexes your spirit, then you should just lower your voice.

Many times, in the services people would stand up in the church to have a word with someone or to tell them off. They would hinder the services and sometimes just turn the service out with their confusion. There were two people that made it a habit of disrupting the services and turning out the services if what was being said or done at the time was not what they wanted done or wanted to hear. But things did begin to change after Mother Grier began teaching the people. And there was an even greater change after Overseer Jones began teaching.

There were mumbling and grumblings behind the Overseer's back, but if the preachers were wrong, she would pull their coat tails and tell them to sit down. Then she would correct the error that the preacher had just committed. She would correct the error in a manner so as not to anger the preacher. Overseer Jones was a leader and a preacher who did not allow error in the church to slide by her. She corrected errors that were taught or preached by the preachers. Even if a visiting preacher were to teach or preach error in the church, she would immediately pull their coat tails and tell them to sit down. Then she would usually get up herself and correct the error. She did not allow error to stand or to take root in the church. After correcting you she would smile with you, eat with you and would not say anything else about it.

Overseer Jones taught the preachers that if you ever start pastoring never let error slip by. For, if error slips by you and stands, then they are taking your authority as the pastor. And you never let anyone come into the church where you pastor and usurp your authority. When someone in the congregation begins to get out of order and uncontrollable, then you sit them down. Otherwise, they have more authority than you do. You must nip the problem in the bud, before it has a chance to grow."

And one point of error, she was determined to correct, involved sickness and the church. She believed that the church was God's hospital and if there was sickness or hurt of any kind God should be allowed the first opportunity to heal, deliver or resurrect, as Apostle James commanded,

> **14 Is any sick among you? let him call for the elders of the church; and let them pray over him, anointing him with oil in the name of the Lord:**
>
> **15 And the prayer of faith shall save the sick, and the Lord shall raise him up; and if he have committed sins, they shall be forgiven him.**
>
> **James 5:14-15.**

GET OUT AND DON'T COME BACK:

THIS IS GOD'S HOSPITAL

For example, on one occasion through Overseer Jones' praying the Lord spared the life of her organ player. His name was Floyd and he was the organist for the Emmanuel Pentecostal

Church located on Warren Street, Lakewood, New Jersey. In addition to being the presiding Chief Overseer of the Emmanuel Pentecostal Churches, Overseer Jones was also the pastor of the Lakewood congregation. On this particular day the organization was hosting a big service where several of the Emmanuel churches were in attendance. The service was in full blast and Floyd was playing the organ. After a while he began to feel bad and so he got up from the organ and left out of the church's main sanctuary and went into the foyer, front vestibule of the church that was located at the church's front entrance. Immediately after Floyd entered the vestibule he passed out of consciousness and fell down on the floor unconscious. He had no body movement and his skin color had changed. He laid there on the floor like a dead man. One of the church deacons, who was also serving as an usher for the service, was standing at the entrance doors when Floyd passed out and fell down. So, the ushering deacon called the other deacons that were in attendance to come and help. No one called for or informed Overseer Jones what had happened, although she was the pastor and she was present at the church.

The deacons gathered around Floyd and tried to revive him by using fans to fan him. Then someone called 911, for emergency services. Still, no one had told Overseer Jones about what had happened to Floyd. But they just decided to call 911. About seven or eight other church members went out into the vestibule to either see what was going on or to offer helping assistance. After a short while the ambulance, rescue squad Emergency Medical Technicians (EMTs) arrived at the church. They came in with their equipment and their bed stretcher. There were two of them. By the time the EMTs were about to place Floyd on the bed stretcher Overseer Jones walked into the vestibule. Then Overseer Jones asked, "What's going on out here?" The deacons began explaining to Overseer Jones that Floyd had passed out of consciousness, had fell down, and how they had not been able to revive him. So they called 911 for emergency services.

By this time the EMTs were placing Floyd on the stretcher and Overseer Jones said to the EMTs, "Put him down! Get your stretcher and get out of here. Put him down! Put him down!" First, the EMTs just looked at Overseer Jones like she was going crazy. She began waving her hands at them and motioning for them to leave, while at the same time saying, "Get out of here! Get out of here!" She told the EMTs, "This is God's church. This is God's house and this is God's hospital. We don't need you here. Take your stretcher and go." By this time, even some of the church members thought that Overseer Jones had lost her mind and was going crazy. They were acting as if no one present believed or understood what she believed and understood about the miraculous power of the Lord Jesus Christ. And to their later surprise the Lord was about to demonstrate his healing and resurrecting power, before them all, through Overseer Jones' faith and prayer.

Overseer Jones was furious and very upset at the way the saved members of the church had behaved—with a lack of faith in the Lord. The EMTs grabbed their equipment and left out of the church vestibule walking backwards so that they could keep their eyes on Overseer Jones. And as they were leaving, she said to them, "Go on and don't come back here anymore!"

Then she turned her attention to Floyd. She ordered everyone to move and get from around Floyd. Then she fell down on her knees and laid over Floyd. While laying over Floyd Overseer began praying to the Lord Jesus on Floyd's behalf. And after a little while, during her praying, those that were watching could see Floyd's skin color changing and coming back to normal. After that he began to move a little bit. When Overseer finished and stopped praying Floyd opened his eyes. Then Overseer ordered the deacons to raise him and pick Floyd up off of the floor. With their help Floyd got up off of the floor and stood on his feet. And, several minutes later Floyd went back into the church, sat at the organ and began playing the organ in a masterful manner like he had never played before.

After ensuring that Floyd was well, Overseer then turned her attention to the deacons that were out in the vestibule. She admonished them not to ever act in such a faithless manner again. She said, "If anybody at this church passes out of consciousness, then you call me. I am the pastor of this church and the church is God's hospital."

I AM DEPENDING ON GOD

Another character trait that assisted Overseer Jones in building and expanding the Emmanuel Pentecostal Church organization to more than 50 churches was the fact that she possessed great, unwavering faith in the Lord Jesus' promises of providing and making provision for the work and ministry of the kingdom of God, and for the spreading of the gospel. For example: The Emmanuel Pentecostal Church organization quickly grew into a Northern and a Southern diocese. Then it became necessary to build a large church facility to host the various conventions and conferences that were being planned, developed and carried out for the organization.

So, as the organization's founder and presiding leader, Overseer Jones spearheaded the building of a headquarters church building to be located and built in Lakewood, New Jersey. She began building the facility knowing that she did not have the funds to finish the job. But she had favor with God. So, she chose her brother, Q.W. Williams, to be the contractor for the new building.

One day while the building was being built and was approximately one half completed something miraculously happened. Overseer Jones, Geneva Mae and several other female Emmanuelites were sitting out in the church yard while the construction workers were working on the building. The women's jobs were to ensure that the workers had water to drink when needed and to basically be construction go-fors for the workers. A construction go-for was someone who brought small items to the workers such as a brick, nail or hammer when they needed or called for them. Geneva Mae was a brick go-for. Whenever Bishop Williams, the contractor needed bricks, Overseer Jones would tell Geneva Mae which bricks to take to him.

On this particular day Overseer was sitting under a tree out in the yard, alone, reading. It was later on in the evening around 3 o'clock in the afternoon. Geneva Mae fetched herself a chair and sat down beside Overseer. Overseer began talking to Geneva Mae about the expense of building the new church and the money that she had to pay out. She said, "These men are here working. I am praying and talking to God. In about an hour and a half from now these men will be done and finished for the day, and they are looking for their pay. I don't have a penny to pay them." Geneva Mae asked, "What are you gonna do?" Overseer replied, "I'm looking for God to provide. I am depending on God and unless God works a miracle there will be no pay for these men today." There she was sitting under the tree with no money to pay the workers for the work that she had hired them to perform. All she had was favor with God and faith in his promises.

Time went by and as it neared quitting time, before the men had stopped working for the day they heard a loud, roaring noise, coming towards them from a distance. The noise sounded like a car that was being driven at a high rate of speed. You could hear the roar of the engine. As the sound got closer Overseer Jones and Geneva Mae began looking in the direction from where the roaring sound was coming from. It came closer and closer, but the women did not know what it was.

Finally, they saw the car coming towards them down Warren Avenue. The driver, whoever it was, seemed to be in a big hurry to reach their destination. The women did not recognize the car and did not know who was driving the car. The driver was driving extremely fast coming down the neighborhood street. The driver drove the car into the church yard while slamming on the brakes to get the car to stop. Then, suddenly a man hurriedly exited the car and hollered saying, "Overseer!" in an excited manner.   Overseer looked at him and the man walked over to where Overseer had been sitting and gave her a big hug. Then he said, "I've got something for you." He then gave Overseer a large sum of money. Upon receiving the money Overseer immediately threw her hands up into the air and began praising the Lord. The man had just received a large, lump sum of money that he had been waiting on. It is reported that he gave Overseer thousands of dollars. Overseer was filled with joy and thanks because the Lord had just shown again his provision power to provide in time of need. For, he had just provided the money needed and required to pay the salaries of the construction laborers before they had stopped and finished working for the day.

EXPANDING THE KINGDOM OF GOD:

GROWING PAINS

With souls being added to the church and some of them entering into the preaching ministry, and with additional churches being added to the Emmanuel organization it became necessary for Overseer Jones to have more help with the administration of the work on a national level. So, on one occasion, in an attempt to address and fulfill this need, during her many visits and travels to North Carolina, Overseer Jones appointed Pastor Ray Ferrens as the National Bishop of the Emmanuel Pentecostal Church organization. This decision, although needful for the proper expansion of the kingdom of God, brought confusion within the young flock of saints that worshiped at the Woodleaf church.

Because, at the time that Pastor Ferrens was appointed as the National Bishop, Deacon James Cowan was also a member of the church and was now also preaching. But he was not chosen.

There Must Be Something To It

During the time that Annie Lee's husband, Nathan King, Sr., sought out salvation through the indwelling Holy Ghost Ray Ferrens was the pastor of the Hart Road congregation. At first, Nathan Sr. was not interested in the church services or what was going on in the services that Mother Grier, Overseer Jones and Ray Ferrens were engaged in primarily for two reasons. First, he attempted to hold onto the Baptist traditions although his wife Annie Lee had forsaken them. And secondly, confusion and jealousy had begun to rear their ugly heads within the congregation of new converts. These concerns became and remained a wall of hindrance to Nathan Sr. until one night when they were traveling from Statesville, North Carolina back to Salisbury and he witnessed his first miracle.

Nathan Sr. grew up in the Baptist church tradition as a member of the New Testament Baptist Church located in Woodleaf, North Carolina, where his mother, Magdaline Woods King's, family were members and attended. His father, Richard Wesley King, did not attend anyone's church. Before the Statesville incident Nathan was attending the services only because his wife Annie Lee had already received the Holy Ghost. And, as a new couple with a one-year-old child, named Nathan Jr., Nathan Sr. wanted to support his wife. So, although he was in attendance at many of the services, he was not paying them any attention. The wall of hindrance gave him his personal justifications for not being interested in the mighty and miraculous work of the Lord that was unfolding right before his eyes.

THE BAPTIST TRADITION PROBLEM

The first problem was that the Baptist folk did things a little different than what he had been witnessing through Mother Grier and those that followed her. And this was partly the same issue that the Baptist members of Shady Grove had also. For salvation, enough to qualify to make it in to heaven's gates, they were taught to repeat Romans 10:9 and were told that they were saved. But, Mother Grier, Overseer Jones and Ray Ferrens all required what the Holy scriptures and the Apostles required—true repentance, water baptism in the name of Jesus Christ and receiving Jesus Christ into your physical body as the indwelling Holy Ghost with the evidence following of speaking in other tongues as the Spirit of God gives utterance.

Nathan Sr. testified, saying, "*In the Baptist church people would get up and shout or dance for the Lord just like the Holiness church, but you never would witness any miracles occurring in the Baptist church. They would have prayer meetings and meetings in the homes also. And people would just come and join the church without changing their lives or their lifestyles. But after I married Annie Lee Mother Grier started coming down and holding services. I would go and sit in the back of the place, wherever they were holding the services, and laugh at them. But whenever this woman, Mother Grier, would start praying you could feel that there was something different. There was something about her praying—it would move you. It was a lot different from what it was like in the Baptist Church, where the ones that prayed would moan and pray, but you would not feel anything from the prayer or the praying. All you would witness was you would see their mouths moving and hear a sound coming out.*

But there was something different about this woman, Mother Hattie Grier. She would pray, crying asking the Lord to save her people.

And yet, although there was a big difference in the power level that you felt from Mother Grier as opposed to those who practiced the Baptist tradition, it still did not move me. In the Baptist church they would cry out and say that they were saved, jump up out of their seats and start dancing for the Lord, hitting you all in the face with their arms and carrying on."

THE CONFUSION PROBLEM

Continuing his testimony, Nathan Sr. stated: *"The next problem that hindered me from getting saved sooner than I did was the confusion that had developed in the new congregation of former Baptist turned Holiness saints. Overseer Jones had come down and promoted Ray Ferrens in the ministry. James Cowan, now a preaching minister was a member of the congregation, but he was not chosen and he felt that he should have been given the position before Ray Ferrens. After all, the growing Woodleaf congregation had its first start in James and Edna Cowan's house. But since he was not chosen James began to talk against the Overseer and Ray Ferrens to the other members of the church and to the family. (And at this time most of the congregation was related in some way.) This caused bad blood to form between Overseer Jones and James Cowan. At times Overseer Jones would make decisions and James would talk against it. (This was how it was done as deacons in the Baptist church.) James would get with us and talk against the Overseer and Ray Ferrens his pastor. It affected the people and hindered the work of the Lord.* (He meant right, but it wasn't right.)

Walter Chambers had received the Holy Ghost also, and was now preaching and pastoring another church. Walter and James were great friends. (Both of them, aWlong with Ray Ferrens, had been members of Shady Grove Baptist Church when Mother Grier conducted the revival there and many souls were baptized and took on the name of Jesus.) *James talked to him and turned Walter against the church leadership, Overseer Jones and Ray Ferrens, for a long time. Because of this bad blood confusion Overseer Jones had a hard time getting things done and straightened out. This is one reason why, even with the demonstration of the power of God that I had witnessed, I was never moved because I said to myself, "All of this type confusion goes on in the Baptist church. So, why should I leave one mess and go into another mess?" It was the same type mess that goes on with the Baptists and now it was going on with the former Baptists in the Holiness church. "*

"But what made me change my mind about the whole thing was the Statesville incident. We were coming from Statesville one night. I was driving. I would always go with them to the prayer meetings and I would drive for Pastor Ferrens. On the way to Salisbury, we ran out of gas up in Cleveland, North Carolina. I allowed the car to roll down the highway as far as it would roll without engine power, before it stopped. Pastor Ferrens got out of the car and asked me to raise the hood on the car. I thought to myself, "We don't have any gas, so why are we raising the hood." He said to me, "Take the breather off of the carburetor." So, out of obedience I took the breather off of the carburetor like he requested. Pastor Ferrens then reached into his coat pocket and pulled out a small bottle of holy, anointing oil." The oil was olive oil. Pastor Ferrens used the oil to anoint people before praying over them, in obedience to the Apostle James' admonition wherein he instructs saying,

> **14 Is any sick among you? let him call for the elders of the church; and let them pray over him, anointing him with oil in the name of the Lord:**

> **15 And the prayer of faith shall   save the sick, and the Lord shall raise him up; and if he have committed sins, they shall be forgiven him.**

> **James 5:14-15.**

The difference here was that, this was a car, a thing and not a person. But that did not prevent Pastor Ferrens from believing in the miraculous power of the Lord Jesus Christ in times of distress and need. *So, he opened the container and poured all of the oil that was left in the bottle into the carburetor. Pastor Ferrens then said to me, "Now get back into the car and crank it up." I got back into the car and turned on the starter ignition to crank the car. The car cranked right up. I drove that car from Cleveland, North Carolina all the way into Salisbury on West Innes Street. At the time there was a Service Distributing, gasoline, filling station across the street from Institute Street, right on West Innes Street. The car cut off right as I approached the gas station. It had enough momentum left to roll up the hill and right up to the gas tanks. The saints that were in the car got out after the car came to a complete stop and glorified God in verbal praise and with the dance right out in the parking lot. It seemed like they danced for about thirty minutes. The people in the gas station saw what was going on in the parking lot with the praises and thought that the saints were going crazy. So, I went home and I thought about that thing. I thought about what had just happened."*

Nathan King Sr. was appointed the State Elder and pastored 4 churches. In 2013 he oversees the new church building project for his son Michael Lee King

SEEING IS BELIEVING

"Pastor Ray Ferrens always conducted Wednesday night prayer meetings. So, the next Wednesday after the healing   oil miracle Pastor Ferrens held a prayer meeting service at a home located in Salisbury. There was a man that worked with us at the treatment plant. His daddy-in-law was lame and had not walked in years. So, Pastor Ferrens took us over to the lame man's house to have a prayer meeting

service. Pastor Ferrrens called him Daddy. He said, "Daddy you are going to walk tonight." It is reported that, at the time, the lame man had not walked for 15 to 20 years. So, Pastor Ferrens prayed. And, during his praying Pastor Ferrens asked the Lord Jesus to heal the lame man on his faith. After the prayer Pastor Ferrens grabbed the lame man by the hand and pulled him up out of his wheel chair. When Pastor Ferrens stood the lame man up his legs were very unstable and they were wobbling like a baby's legs wobble when they first attempt to walk. Seeing this, Pastor Ferrens turned the lame man's hands a loose and left the man standing there. Pastor Ferrens backed away from the lame man and said, "Daddy, make a step!"

Up until this time I had been sitting in my seat and looking. But, by now I had gotten up out of my seat. I said to myself, "I'm gonna see this." The lame man put his leg out and it looked as if he was going to fall. Pastor Ferrens, looked at the lame man and backed further away from him. Then he said, "Daddy, make another step." The lame man put his other leg out in front of him. Pastor Ferrens said, "Lord, heal him on my faith!" Pastor Ferrens then backed away as far as he could get from the man—all the way to the farthest back wall of the living room. Then, Pastor Ferrens said, "Come and grab my hand Daddy." The lame man then walked over to Pastor Ferrens and grabbed the Pastor's hand. I was looking at this because I knew the lame man. Many times, when I would go by to pick up his son-in-law to provide him a ride to work, the son-in-law would be in the process of lifting the lame man off of his bed, carrying him and placing him into a chair. This prayer service was in the living room of the house where the lame man lived.

After he grabbed Pastor Ferrens' hand, the lame man began running around and around in the living room. The next morning when we went by to give the son-in-law a ride, we discovered that the lame man was sitting out on the front porch of the house. I asked the son-in-law, "Is the old man still walking?" The son-in-law answered, "Yes! He's still walking and he just completed walking around the block and came back and sat on the porch. Now he's waiting on his *breakfast." I saw that! This miracle is another thing that caused me to start thinking that, "If God can do that, then there is something to this new doctrine and manner of living that they had been preaching and teaching about."*

"At first I did not believe that there was anything to this new doctrine. When my wife Annie Lee would get ready to go to church, I would say to her, "I'll take you, or I'll go with you." I would go with her, but I would sit all the way in the back of the church laughing at the holiness church folk. But now, I had finally witnessed some things that made me realize that there is a God. And so, after being an eyewitness to these miracles, from then on when I would go to the church, I made a decision that I would go to the front of the church and sit down. "

THE NIGHT I RECEIVED THE INDWELLING HOLY GHOST

"The night that I received the gift of the indwelling Holy Ghost, Overseer Jones was present. On this particular night Overseer Jones was conducting a revival. She had come down from New Jersey. When the altar call was made, I went to the altar. But before I knelt down at the altar, I said to myself, "I'm gonna get the Holy Ghost tonight."

After I knelt down on the altar Overseer Jones obtained a straight chair and sat down right in front of me at the altar. I could hear her voice. She was saying, "Call him baby. He's right at the tip of your tongue. Call him baby." Then after a while, all at once it seemed like something picked me up and carried me down in the bottom all by myself. While in this place I could not hear the Overseer or anybody else. All I remember is that something grabbed me and picked me up. Later, I opened my eyes and looked down. I was trying to stop my feet from moving, but they would not stop. From my waistline on down I was moving. I was trying to say something to the Overseer, but my mouth was saying something else. I heard the Overseer say, "Baby you've got it." Then the Overseer began praising and glorifying God with the dance. And then the others in attendance began praising and glorifying God with the dance. That was a time. I'll tell anybody, there is no time like that of receiving the indwelling Holy Ghost. I received the gift of the Holy Ghost after 12 o'clock midnight in the wee hours of the night. Everyone else that had been on the altar or was helping on the altar had long ago taken their seats or had left the little old school house for the night. But the Overseer sat right there, by the altar, with me until I came through speaking in tongues as the Spirit of God gave me utterance.

When I was calling on Jesus and the Holy Ghost came upon me—it was like someone had pulled up in a car or other vehicle. And there was a real cool wind surrounding me. I do not believe that I would have received salvation by getting the Holy Ghost if I had not witnessed the working of the miracles. When I saw the miracles I knew then, that there was something to this preaching and teaching about receiving salvation by repenting of one's sins, being baptized in water in the name of Jesus Christ and receiving the indwelling Holy Ghost."

James Cowan left Emmanuel, built a new church and served as a bishop in another church organization.

After securing his salvation at Mother Grier's feet, Robert O. Doubs went on to become pastor founder and Bishop of Shiloh Apostolic Temple.

Bishop Walter Chambers became the Southern Diocese Bishop of the Emmanuel Pentecostal Church. Upon leaving Emmanuel his congregation split and he built a new church.

Bishop David Chambers pastors the new church that his father, Walter Chambers built on Sandra Avenue.

Bishop Arthur Wayne Brown, cousin of Elder Leroy Mills, pastors the Smith's Chapel Church, at Amity Hill.

Sister Christine Cornelious, age 93 in 2013, remains of sound mind and a great Evangelist for the Lord Jesus

Hattie McAfee pastored the Spratt Street congregation after Mother Hattie Grier moved to Philadelphia Pennsylvania permanently in 1946.

Bishop Robert Lee Huey, Jr. is the pastor of the congregation that Mother Grier and Pastor McAfee started on Spratt Street, Charlotte, NC. He is also the presiding Bishop over the corporate work, left behind by Pastor McAfee.

I Have Finished My Course
A Miracle Even In Death

The day did not seem right. It did not start right and so it did not end right. Mother Grier had celebrated only 61 years of life on this earth. And for the last several years of that life she had night and day warned her friends, family and everyone else that would listen, that the wages of sin were death, but the gift of God was eternal life. By 1964 she had been preaching for more than 20 years. The Lord Jesus had worked so many miracles through her and so many people had come to know the Lord because of the obedience in her own life. Although, she would not be around in this life to see it, God had not stopped working miracles through her obedience to him. But now, Mother Grier was lying in the hospital with cancer that had developed from a soft tissue injury about a year prior. According to the doctors the cancer came about as a result of injuries sustained in a car accident.

At this time Mother Grier was separated from her husband, Earl Grier, and was living with her son, James Luckey, in Williamstown, New Jersey. Those that knew James called him by his sir name, Luckey. Luckey had driven Mother Grier to see her brother Theodore 'Pete' Caldwell in Washington D. C. On the way back from Washington, D. C. Luckey had stopped at a red lighted intersection and was waiting for the light to change. They had not made it back to Philadelphia. They were sitting there at the light in Bear, Delaware, when suddenly and without warning, another car approaching the intersection from behind Luckey's car failed to see Luckey's car stopped at the red light. And, with a force of great impact the negligent driver plowed his automobile directly into the rear-end of Luckey's car. Luckey's car was badly damaged, but he was able to get it back home. Mother Grier had been riding in the back seat of the car, and the soft tissue of her body absorbed the force of the tremendous impact. Mother Grier was taken to the hospital by ambulance and was checked by the doctors on duty. The doctors did not find any obvious, broken, fractures or lacerated injuries during the examination. So, everyone assumed that, besides the bruises and soreness that Mother Grier felt, she would soon be okay. Mother Grier was paid well by her son's insurance company—well enough to buy herself a brand new, station wagon car.

Sometime after the accident, Mother Grier moved from Luckey's house to live with Geneva Mae at 2469 Douglas Street, Philadelphia, Pennsylvania. Geneva Mae helped Mother Grier by hiring her as a live-in nanny to take care of her two, small children, Derrick and Beverly, while Geneva Mae worked. This arrangement worked out well. And for a while, it seemed like everything would be okay. But several months after Mother Grier had settled with the insurance company, she began to hurt and feel pain in her lower back, thigh, hip and buttocks area. At first the pain was on and then off, on then off. Mother Grier visited her doctors and he gave her pads and other medications and ointments to rub her body down, in an attempt to treat the condition. But it did not help with keeping the pain away. The pain gradually got worse and worse, until Mother Grier was not able to walk or to get around unassisted.

Finally, the pain grew so intense and her movements became so limited that Mother Grier was admitted to the hospital as an in-patient. Her doctors began conducting various tests trying to pinpoint the problem. And, eventually, the doctors became the messengers of bad news. It was now more than a year since the accident. But the doctors informed Mother Grier that the accident had caused soft tissue injuries that could not have been detected during the time of the accident. And now, many, many months later, the injury had become a malignant cancerous site within her hip. This is the area of her body that had absorbed the impact and had suffered the major soft tissue injuries during the errant automobile's tumultuous impact.

After Mother Grier was admitted into the hospital, she was there for only a short while before she passed. Her mind was good and sharp, and at first so was her will to get up and run on for the Lord. Even the initial instructions that she had given Geneva Mae revealed a mind to fight and to run on in this life and to continue her work for the Lord. After all, she was only 61 years old, nine years short of the 70 that the Lord had promised and 19 years short of the 80 that he had promised for strength. Mother Grier believed that God would heal her of the cancer if she asked him. So, at this time she was not looking to go home to be with the Lord. She was looking and preparing to live on, to work on winning souls for the kingdom of God.

Mother Hattie Mae Grier had instructed Geneva Mae to go to the Catholic, second-hand thrift store and tell a Ms. Collins, the manager of the store, to give her a bed for Mother Grier. Ms. Collins knew Mother Grier, because Mother Grier was a regular customer of the store. She knew Mother Grier so well until she knew all of her children's names and genders and what type of things Mother Grier liked to buy for them, and for her grandchildren. Although all of Mother Grier's children were grown, she still bought things for them, because she loved her children. Ms. Collins liked Mother Grier. So, when she would see things in the store that she thought Mother Grier would like for herself, her children or her grandchildren, Ms. Collins would put those items aside for Mother Grier and keep them off of the sales floor until Mother Grier could get by to see them. Ms. Collins even knew the days that Mother Grier would come to shop at the store.

Mother Grier continued with her instructions telling Geneva Mae, "I want you to take the bed and set it up inside the church. After you have set the bed up inside the church, I want you to call all of the Elders and Bishops and tell them that I want them to meet me at the church that they may lay hands on me so that I may be healed, as the bible says. For, in the book of James chapter 5, verses 14 and 15, it does say,

Is any sick among you? let him call for the elders of the church; and let them pray over him, anointing him with oil in the name of the Lord: And the prayer of faith shall save the sick, and the Lord shall raise him up...

When Geneva Mae first called Ms. Collins, she could not reach her. But, when she finally did get in touch with Ms. Collins, Geneva Mae told her about Mother Grier's request for the bed. Ms. Collins, saddened by the news of Mother Grier's condition, readily agreed to provide the bed.

But, strangely, several days after Mother Grier had instructed Geneva Mae to prepare the way and means for her healing which would have resulted in her return to the work of the Lord, she had a change of heart. On this fateful day the friends, saints and family came by to wish her a speedy recovery because they were aware of her desire and belief that God would heal her of the cancer if she asked him, and of her plans to have the Elders and Bishops anoint her with oil, lay hands and pray over her. However, on this day she arranged, with the hospital staff, for Geneva Mae to remain with her after the visiting hours were over and all of her other visitors had gone home. The hospital normally would not have allowed it, but Mother Grier told them, "Geneva Mae is not the pastor of my church. I am. But she is my daughter. She is my assistant in the church and I need to talk to her about the church and the things that I want her to do. Will you allow her to stay?" The hospital staff agreed and Geneva Mae hung around after all of Mother Grier's other visitors had gone home.

After the room was empty of all uninvited ears Mother Grier said to Geneva Mae, "Since you are the only one of my children that has not backslid into sin, I want you to do all that you can to keep the church going on. I have lived the way God told me to live and I did what God told me to do. I'm ready to go home." Geneva Mae, unaware and unsuspecting that Mother Grier had changed her mind about being healed, thought that the reference to 'going home' referred to going back to Geneva Mae's house since Mother Grier had been living with her. So, Geneva Mae let her know that she could go home and that it was alright for her to come back to her house. Mother Grier realizing that Geneva Mae did not understand exactly what home she was referring to cleared up the misunderstanding by saying, "No. I am not talking about your house. I am ready to go home to be with the Lord." Geneva Mae, shocked and dismayed, exclaimed, "Mama how can you talk like that?" Geneva Mae's heart had suddenly become extra heavy after receiving this totally unsuspected, heart numbing, news update. And this weighted down heart brought tears to her eyes. In a slight stutter, Geneva Mae gently reminded her mother of the earlier arrangements that she had made, saying, "You, you told me to call Ms. Collins and…" Mother Grier cut her off in midsentence, not allowing her to finish, and said to her anxious and now sorrowfully, excited daughter, "Yea. I know I did, but I changed my mind." Gazing at her daughter she said again, "I did what God told me to do. And he told me that if I would live right, he would save my family. She said God has brought almost all of my children into the church. And those that are not in, they are coming because God promised me that."

After allowing Geneva Mae a few moments to process the worst news that she had ever heard; news that was monumentally worse than the news of her exile to Philadelphia with no return to Charlotte, North Carolina, some years ago, Mother Grier continued saying, "I have even asked God to allow someone to get saved at my funeral." Her words dropped upon Geneva Mae's emotional frame like a ton of bricks falling upon a single, crystal glass sitting in the middle of a deserted highway, miles away from the hearing of the nearest human ear. Um. It struck like a dead, thud thump. This last piece of information was completely over the top. It was too much news. It was more than Geneva Mae wanted to hear and more than she wanted to know. It was news that had been intentionally scrapped naked from any inkling of hope, hope for even the remotest chance of healing. Faith for healing was told to stand down. No healing is desired. Leave faith. Vacate the premises and do not look back. Geneva Mae was not ready for this part of God's plan and will. Her mother and God were in cahoots in getting Mother Grier out of this life and into the next. She had run her race with patience. She had finished her course. It was now time to be offered up and to take her final rest in Him.

Then, like a tornado spun from a raging hurricane at sea, reality set in. Geneva Mae was hit with grief, anguish, sorrow and ignorance of God's will, all in the same thunderbolt of time. It clobbered her heart. Geneva Mae was now 35 years old, but it did not matter. The sea of tears came from within; gushing out from her eyes like a river whose banks had been breached and who's over flow could not be stopped. She could not hold it in. Her mother had given up and changed her mind concerning the healing process. Here she was lying there. God was able to heal her, but she desired not to be healed that she may leave her body and thereby leave them. It was too much. They needed her. She needed her. At 35 and alone with two small children, how could she carry on? Geneva Mae thought. Momma Hattie Mae had always been there for the good, for the bad. Always!

The light of the room now caused the rivers of sorrow to glisten and glow as they drained down her still smooth, dark cheeks into her pitiful lap. Momma is leaving us she thought. Geneva Mae was ignorant of the spiritual side of what the Lord was doing. She did not understand and right then at that moment, she was not trying to understand, did not want to understand. All she knew was that her mother, the woman that had birthed her; the woman that had suffered so much to get them up; the woman that had traveled more than 500 miles from her own birth place to make a complete change of address just to save her from herself, that she might have a better life—had now decided to leave her on this earth without a mother. It really was more than Geneva Mae thought that she could bare. The tears were driven out of her eyes by the immensity of her hurt and open sorrow. This was all unexpected. It was like witnessing her mother's death, in slow motion, in a movie preview days before the movie plays. Not even the doctors were expecting what was coming down in just a few days. And, no one else expected Mother Grier to pass away as quick as she did.

In an attempt to assist her daughter in the processing and handling of the news of her soon, coming death, Mother Grier tried to encourage her. She said, "Geneva Mae, you do everything that you can to keep the church going on. And if you will be faithful to God, he will surely bless you. I want you to do everything that you can so that you and my children can stay together."

And as she had promised, she went home. A mere several days later the Lord dispatched the angel of death to come and take her home to the place that she had so many times preached about and told so many others within her hearing to prepare themselves to go. Elder Mother Hattie Mae Grier, while residing at 2469 Douglas Street, Philadelphia, Pennsylvania with her daughter, Geneva Mae Adams, left this life on Sunday, the 5th day of April, 1964. At the tender age of 61 she left behind a legacy of work for the Lord, a separated husband, Earl Grier, and eleven children namely: Percy, Christine, Eldora, James, Louise, June, Geneva Mae, Leola, Johnsie Bea, Delphine and Hattie, 58 grandchildren and 7 great grandchildren. Additionally, she was survived by five brothers, Pete, Ray, Ralph, Fred and Everett and two sisters, Edna and Ruth. Preceding her in death was one child, Floyd, two brothers, Chad and James, and two sisters, Lucille and Emma.

By the time Mother Grier departed this life, her work had touched many hearts and souls, in the North and the South. Two 'Going Home Services', on her behalf, were conducted. Of course, this is what Mother Grier wanted because she had made her own funeral arrangements before she ever got sick. She often talked about things that she had learned from her Jewish employers. And one of those things was that a person should not wait until death to make their funeral arrangements. Because, a dead person cannot talk or make decisions. A person should make their decisions concerning their funeral and how they want it conducted while they are alive. Mother Grier believed this. So, that is what she did. One service was held in Philadelphia where the Chief Overseer Carrie Francis Jones delivered the eulogy. During the eulogy Overseer Jones styled Mother Grier as a General Motors Cadillac that had been engaged in a test drive all during her life. And at the end, when her fenders, doors, tires and bumpers had fallen off, with nothing left but the engine, the Lord Jesus, owner of her soul (the engine) instructed his workers to bring the soul back home, because it belonged to him.

The second service was held at the family's home church called Mt. Zion Baptist Church, Boyden Quarters. Mt. Zion, a church that was founded during slavery in 1853, is located in Mt. Ulla, Rowan County, North Carolina on White Road. Although many of the people objected, the teaching while preaching Bishop L. R. Mills, conducted the eulogy. At this time the fellowship between the churches in North Carolina and Bishop Mills' organization had cooled down due to the religious, political trouble. But it was fitting and proper for Bishop Mills to deliver

Mother Grier's eulogy, since it was through his preaching and teaching that Mother Grier had met the Lord Jesus Christ. And it was her obedience to this teaching and preaching and her belief in the cleansing, delivering, healing and salvational power of the blood of Christ that had changed her life so dramatically. Yes, it had taken 'a sack full of blood' shed on Calvary's Cross from the death of a man who loved her, who rose again on the third day morning never to die again; who, after having been invited in, came to live within her, and now had taken her home.

It was Elder L. R. Mills, now elevated to the office of bishop, who had introduced her to a life in Christ Jesus. And now it would be Bishop L. R. Mills who would honor her by giving her departed spirit and her lifeless body a going home service befitting a soldier who had died on the battle field on her way to glory.

And, for one last time, the Lord Jesus Christ answered her prayer, even in death. While the undertaker was lowering Mother Grier's lifeless body down into its final resting place, as her body reached about halfway down into the grave hole, Luckey's wife, Rose, began shaking, crying out and saying thank you Jesus. At the time, Luckey nor Rose was saved, but Rose had been on the altar seeking the Lord and the infilling of the Holy Ghost. She had come to the altar often while in Philadelphia at Mother Grier's church. While she was saying, "Thank you Jesus", the power of the Lord fell upon her and she fell down. The power was so strong until it shook her. The people who did not personally know Rose or who had not personally had the Day of Pentecost experience thought that Rose was having a seizure or something or that she was just grief stricken. After all, Mother Grier had been a wonderful Mother-in-law to her. And she had lived with them for a long spell after Mother Grier's separation from Earl Grier. But that was not the case. To see it, it looked as if an invisible person was just knocking her down every time she would try to get up. And as she was knocked down, she would holler Jesus. Then she began speaking in stammering tongues. It was obvious to those who were of the Pentecostal experience that Rose had just received the indwelling Holy Ghost. They gathered Rose up and took her to the car. And with excited joy at what had just happened and with an anxious anticipation of more to come later, Mother Grier's family left the grave site at Mt. Zion Baptist Church, Boyden Quarters and went to her sister Edna Cowan's house. After arriving at Sister Edna's house, the group that assembled there had church all over again, right there in the house and Rose began speaking in a more fluent, foreign tongue. It was a beautiful sight to behold, to see and be a witness to the power of God taking control of this woman's life. And Geneva Mae, remembering what her mother had told her at her hospital bedside, thought, yes, even in death, the Lord has answered Momma's prayer. Someone, not her son Luckey, but his wife Rose, had received the indwelling Spirit of the Lord Jesus Christ at Mother Grier's funeral.

THE ALCOHOLIC DEMON CAST OUT

Yes, the Lord Jesus did a mighty work, in the land, through the labor of Mother Hattie Grier's life, and walk of faith. And, He performed many noted miracles to assist Mother Grier in her evangelistic work for Him, like the time when she cast the demonic spirit out of an uncontrollable alcoholic.

During this occasion, Mother Grier's brother, Pete, had married a woman who went by the name of Mary. Mary was a tall, brown skinned beauty of a woman. Her physical looks were very pleasant to the eyes. Pete and Mary had moved to Washington, D.C. And, after having settled in really well and living the life in the D.C. world, Mary began frequently drinking and then abusing alcoholic beverages. She drank so much and so often until she could no longer control her drinking and she became an alcoholic drinker without any temperance or self-control. After a long period of daily abusing alcoholic beverages, Mary's sickness grew worse and her condition during these times was such that she appeared to be demon possessed. With no one else to turn to, Brother Pete called upon Mother Grier for assistance and prayer for his beloved wife, Mary. Mother Grier, a praying, preaching, prayer warrior did not hesitate. Mary's soul was at stake and Mother Grier was an evangelist engaged in the business of rescuing and saving souls. So, Mother Grier prayed the prayer of faith and the Lord Jesus healed Mary of her condition. Mary did fine for a long time. But as time went on she slipped back into her old ways and began sipping on the alcoholic bottle again. And as before, her condition became such that she was visibly sick and tormented because of the alcohol. Brother Pete called Mother Grier a second time and again Mother Grier prayed the prayer of faith and Mary recovered and did well for a long time once again.

And finally, the third time came when Mary, who at one time had once possessed show stopping beauty, had seemingly come to the end of her sojourn and existed in a helpless state; nursing that mean, old alcoholic demon that was visibly tormenting her and making her sick. Brother Pete, unable to sit idly by and watch his beloved Mary wither away in such a pitiful and useless state called upon Mother Grier for a third and final time. When she received the call, Mother Grier informed Brother Pete that this time, Mary would have to leave Washington, D.C. and come to Philadelphia, Pennsylvania to live with Mother Grier for a while. Mother Grier told Brother Pete that Mary was possessed by an alcoholic, drinking, demonic spirit and that that demonic spirit would have to be cast out of her. This was necessary, because, over a period of four or five years Mary's condition had progressively and visibly grown worse. Mary absolutely could not control her urge, her will or her desire to abusively consume alcoholic drinks.

So, with her mission of rescue and deliverance in mind, Mother Grier fetched Mary from Brother Pete's house in Washington, D.C. and moved Mary, temporarily to Philadelphia, to stay with her. After arriving in Philadelphia Mother Grier sat down with Mary and counseled her with the Word of God. During the counseling session Mother Grier told Mary that, "The Lord is going to deliver you. This makes the third time that He would have healed and delivered you from this same thing. Now, after you are delivered this time, if you go back to your drinking alcoholic beverages again, there will be no cure, no healing and no deliverance for you." Mary acknowledged that she understood the consequences of returning to her old life-style after being healed. She wanted to be delivered.

And, one day, after Mary had lived with Mother Grier for a while, in Philadelphia, Mother Grier began the process of casting out the demonic spirit that had held Mary as its captive to abusing alcoholic drinks, for so long. Mother Grier prayed for Mary and took her hands and placed them around Mary's neck and throat. Mother Grier cast out the demon by first binding the alcoholic demon in the name of Jesus Christ. Then she commanded the demon to come out of Mary and leave in the name of Jesus. After Mother Grier had commanded the demonic spirit to leave, Mary's mouth flew wide open as if someone had taken their hands and forcefully opened her mouth wide very quickly. To a bystander it appeared that once Mary's mouth flew wide open something came out and left her body. After this force left Mary's body Mary's body immediately went limp. The force that had filled it up and caused it to stand up in a rigid fashion had now exited her body through her mouth. It was like a blown-up balloon, first full of air, then popped and now it lay flat and deflated. And now, with nothing left to prop her limp body up, Mary immediately, with the force and thump of a dead woman falling down, fell down on the floor of Mother Grier's house like a cooked, string of spaghetti. Mary laid in the same spot, motionlessly, just like that lifeless string of spaghetti, for a while—like a dead woman. And then, as if she had been dead but now had been revived with life, Mary raised herself up off of the floor. She got up and once she became sure footed again, she immediately began rejoicing and praising God for her deliverance. She had been out of her mind. But now Mary was back. She had regained control of her will, her urges, her desires and her mind.

Mary stayed with Mother Grier for about a week or two longer, after her deliverance from the demon. She later went back to Washington, D.C. to her husband and her home. On this third time around Mary did very well. When Mary returned home, she was fully back to herself and began going back to church. Now, she was normal again without the alcohol, without the demonic possession.

The Lord Jesus healed many other people of various diseases through Mother Grier's prayers of faith, including the dreaded disease called Leukemia.

To ensure that her work was carried on, the daughter that Mother Grier had set out to save from herself between the years of 1945-1946, Geneva Mae, now a preaching mother herself, took up the mantle and eventually became the pastor of Mother Grier's church congregation. And, of course at this time, the church had become a sister church within the Emmanuel Pentecostal Church of Our Lord of the Apostolic Faith, Inc., church organization. But the new pastor wanted a name change for the church congregation to honor the great work that Elder Mother Grier had done, over the years, for the Lord. So, in consultation with Emmanuel's presiding founder and Chief Overseer Carrie F. Jones, the church congregation became known as the Emmanuel Grier Memorial Pentecostal Church.

About the Author

Michael is the third child of two preachers, Annie Lee King and Nathan King, Sr., who were also his first tutors in the ways of the Lord Jesus. Having been nurtured in the ways and admonition of the Lord from his youth, he was educated in the Rowan County, North Carolina public school system. Michael earned his Bachelor of Arts degree in Music Education from North Carolina Central University in 1982, with honors. After passing the National Teachers Examination and receiving an 'A Certificate' to teach in the public schools from the State of North Carolina, Michael taught in the Warren County public school system in 1982-1983. He graduated again with honors in 1986 from the North Carolina Central University School of Law, Durham, North Carolina, with a Juris Doctorate Degree.

Michael met Christ Jesus, while attending law school in 1984, the same year that he married Angela Culbertson. He has been a father to seven children and grandfather to four. In 1998, after recognizing the call into the preaching ministry, he received further instruction from Elder C.F. Jones Jackson, Elder Ivey L. Cowan and later from Dr. Gregg Singer upon enrolling in the Southeastern Theological Seminary, Atlanta, Georgia.

Michael has published and written legal articles, religious skits and plays, songs and autobiographies in addition to the four-volume book series, 'The Greatest Mystery Ever Revealed: The Mystery of the Will of God: *Book One:* The Image of God; *Book Two:* Growing in Grace; *Book Three:* The Obedience of Faith; and *Book Four:* The Mystery of Satan—Believing Warriors in Combat.' Michael has traveled widely and hosted two regular radio programs. He laid the foundation for Damascus Church in 1989, and in

1992, the Chief Overseer, Elder C.F. Jones Jackson elevated him to the National Board of the Emmanuel Churches worldwide. In the year 2000, as a bishop for the Emmanuel Churches, Bishop King began performing extensive evangelism and missionary work in the poor areas of North Carolina, USA, Alabama, USA, and in South Africa. Michael presently pastors Damascus Church, of the Emmanuel Churches, performs the bishopric duties for the churches founded by Bishop Leroy R. Mills in Florida, USA, and works in a teaching fellowship with Bishop Robert Lee Huey, Jr., Charlotte, North Carolina, USA.

www.ingramcontent.com/pod-product-compliance
Lightning Source LLC
Chambersburg PA
CBHW022104050726
47591CB00002B/670